I0411842

EXECUTIVE BRANCH STAND-ARDS FOR LAND-IN-TRUST DECISIONS FOR GAMING PURPOSES

OVERSIGHT HEARING

BEFORE THE

SUBCOMMITTEE ON INDIAN AND ALASKA NATIVE AFFAIRS

OF THE

COMMITTEE ON NATURAL RESOURCES
U.S. HOUSE OF REPRESENTATIVES

ONE HUNDRED THIRTEENTH CONGRESS

FIRST SESSION

Thursday, September 19, 2013

Serial No. 113–42

Printed for the use of the Committee on Natural Resources

Available via the World Wide Web: http://www.fdsys.gov
or
Committee address: http://naturalresources.house.gov

U.S. GOVERNMENT PRINTING OFFICE

82–949 PDF   WASHINGTON : 2014

For sale by the Superintendent of Documents, U.S. Government Printing Office
Internet: bookstore.gpo.gov   Phone: toll free (866) 512–1800; DC area (202) 512–1800
Fax: (202) 512–2104   Mail: Stop IDCC, Washington, DC 20402–0001

COMMITTEE ON NATURAL RESOURCES

DOC HASTINGS, WA, *Chairman*
PETER A. DeFAZIO, OR, *Ranking Democratic Member*

Don Young, AK
Louie Gohmert, TX
Rob Bishop, UT
Doug Lamborn, CO
Robert J. Wittman, VA
Paul C. Broun, GA
John Fleming, LA
Tom McClintock, CA
Glenn Thompson, PA
Cynthia M. Lummis, WY
Dan Benishek, MI
Jeff Duncan, SC
Scott R. Tipton, CO
Paul A. Gosar, AZ
Raúl R. Labrador, ID
Steve Southerland, II, FL
Bill Flores, TX
Jon Runyan, NJ
Mark E. Amodei, NV
Markwayne Mullin, OK
Chris Stewart, UT
Steve Daines, MT
Kevin Cramer, ND
Doug LaMalfa, CA
Jason T. Smith, MO

Eni F. H. Faleomavaega, AS
Frank Pallone, Jr., NJ
Grace F. Napolitano, CA
Rush Holt, NJ
Raúl M. Grijalva, AZ
Madeleine Z. Bordallo, GU
Jim Costa, CA
Gregorio Kilili Camacho Sablan, CNMI
Niki Tsongas, MA
Pedro R. Pierluisi, PR
Colleen W. Hanabusa, HI
Tony Cárdenas, CA
Steven A. Horsford, NV
Jared Huffman, CA
Raul Ruiz, CA
Carol Shea-Porter, NH
Alan S. Lowenthal, CA
Joe Garcia, FL
Matt Cartwright, PA
Vacancy

Todd Young, *Chief of Staff*
Lisa Pittman, *Chief Legislative Counsel*
Penny Dodge, *Democratic Staff Director*
David Watkins, *Democratic Chief Counsel*

————

SUBCOMMITTEE ON INDIAN AND ALASKA NATIVE AFFAIRS

DON YOUNG, AK, *Chairman*
COLLEEN W. HANABUSA, HI, *Ranking Democratic Member*

Dan Benishek, MI
Paul A. Gosar, AZ
Markwayne Mullin, OK
Steve Daines, MT
Kevin Cramer, ND
Doug LaMalfa, CA
Doc Hastings, WA, *ex officio*

Tony Cárdenas, CA
Raul Ruiz, CA
Eni F. H. Faleomavaega, AS
Raúl M. Grijalva, AZ
Peter A. DeFazio, OR, *ex officio*

————

(II)

CONTENTS

OVERSIGHT HEARING ON EXECUTIVE BRANCH STANDARDS FOR LAND-IN-TRUST DECISIONS FOR GAMING PURPOSES

Thursday, September 19, 2013
U.S. House of Representatives
Subcommittee on Indian and Alaska Native Affairs
Committee on Natural Resources
Washington, DC

The subcommittee met, pursuant to notice, at 2:19 p.m., in room 1334, Longworth House Office Building, Hon. Don Young [Chairman of the Subcommittee] presiding.

Present: Representatives Young, Mullin, Cramer, LaMalfa, Hanabusa, Cárdenas, Ruiz, and DeFazio.

Mr. YOUNG. The Subcommittee on Indian and Alaska Native Affairs is meeting today to hear testimony on executive branch standards for land-in-trust decisions for gaming purposes.

Under Committee rule 4(f), opening statements are limited to myself and the Ranking Member of the Subcommittee. However, I ask unanimous consent to include any other Members' opening statements in the hearing record, if submitted to the clerk by the close of business today.

[No response.]

Mr. YOUNG. Hearing no objection, so ordered. I will recognize myself.

STATEMENT OF THE HON. DON YOUNG, A REPRESENTATIVE IN CONGRESS FROM THE STATE OF ALASKA

Mr. YOUNG. The purpose of today's hearing is to broadly examine the administration's process for approving gaming rights on lands acquired in trust after 1988. To simplify the discussion of a complex issue for the purpose of this hearing, I will use the term "off-reservation gaming" to refer to tribal gaming conducted pursuant to any exemptions in Section 20(b) of the Indian Gaming Regulatory Act.

I have always been a strong advocate of Indian gaming. Indeed, I was the Ranking Republican Member on the Interior Committee that drafted and passed the Indian Gaming Regulatory Act, which was signed by President Ronald Reagan on October 17, 1988. Tribal gaming has been one of the most successful revenue generators for tribal governments, and has raised the standard of living for many tribal communities in most regions of the United States. It is because of my support for protecting the integrity of tribal gaming that I scheduled this hearing.

The BIA's recent approval, some say, rubber-stamp, of certain trust land applications over the objections of other tribes and surrounding communities, is causing public support to erode for tribal gaming. Many tribes are currently operating successful facilities on their own reservations, in accordance to IGRA. However, the BIA is approving off-reservation facilities that threaten the viability of these existing operations. It is remarkable how tone-deaf the administration has been, and concerns expressed by Members of Congress, Indian Tribes, and other government officials regarding the impacts of off-reservation casinos.

A number of Indian tribes understand what's at stake. They are requesting reasonable policy changes. The more that BIA approves off-reservation projects, the more that existing tribal operations are harmed. And more States are encouraged to authorize private competition in urban areas, which may drain revenues from tribal casinos. In this kind of scenario, who wins? It isn't going to be the tribes. It should be the intention of this committee to consider reforming Federal gaming policy to address growing opposition to off-reservation gaming so as to avoid a backlash that might reverse the gains that Indian Country fight for, and won, when IGRA was enacted.

The passage of a House bill this week to block off-reservation casinos in Phoenix is a sign of popular support of taking the off-reservation gaming rubber stamp away from the administration, and letting Congress make decisions regarding gaming.

And I would yield to the Ranking Member at this time.

[The prepared statement of Mr. Young follows:]

PREPARED STATEMENT OF THE HONORABLE DON YOUNG, CHAIRMAN, SUBCOMMITTEE ON INDIAN AND ALASKA NATIVE AFFAIRS

The purpose of today's hearing is to broadly examine the administration's process for approving gaming rights on lands acquired in trust after 1988.

To simplify the discussion of a complex issue, for the purpose of this hearing I will use the term "off-reservation gaming" to refer to tribal gaming conducted pursuant to any of the exceptions in section 20(b) of the Indian Gaming Regulatory Act.

I have always been a strong advocate of Indian gaming. Indeed, I was the Ranking Republican Member of the Interior Committee which drafted and passed the Indian Gaming Regulatory Act, which was signed by President Ronald Reagan on October 17, 1988.

Tribal gaming has been one of the most successful revenue generators for tribal governments and it has raised the standard of living for many tribal communities in most regions of the United States.

It is because of my support for protecting the integrity of tribal gaming that I scheduled this hearing. The BIA's recent approval—some would say "rubber-stamping" —of certain trust land applications over the objections of other tribes and surrounding communities is causing public support to erode for tribal gaming.

Many tribes are currently operating successful facilities on their own reservations in accordance with IGRA. However, the BIA is approving off-reservation facilities that threaten the viability of these existing operations.

It is remarkable how tone-deaf the administration has been to concerns expressed by Members of Congress, Indian tribes, and other government officials regarding the impacts of off-reservation casinos. A number of Indian tribes understand what is at stake, and they are requesting reasonable policy changes.

The more that BIA approves off-reservation projects, the more that existing tribal operations are harmed, and the more States are encouraged to authorize private competition in urban areas, which may drain revenues from tribal casinos.

In this kind of scenario, who wins? It isn't the tribes.

It should be the objective of this committee to consider reforming Federal gaming policy to address growing opposition to off-reservation gaming so as to avoid a backlash that might reverse the gains that Indian Country fought for and won when IGRA was enacted.

The passage of a House bill this week to block an off-reservation casino in Phoenix is a sign of popular support for taking the off-reservation gaming rubber stamp away from the administration, and letting Congress make decisions regarding gaming.

STATEMENT OF THE HON. COLLEEN W. HANABUSA, A REPRESENTATIVE IN CONGRESS FROM THE STATE OF HAWAII

Ms. HANABUSA. Thank you, Mr. Chairman, for holding today's oversight hearing on the executive branch standards for placing land in trust for gaming purposes.

As this subcommittee is well aware, gaming has provided economic opportunities for Indian tribes that, prior to the passage of the Indian Gaming Regulation Act, IGRA, in 1988, were practically unimaginable. According to the National Indian Gaming Commission, in 2012 alone, revenues generated by the Indian gaming industry totaled $27.9 billion. These are the highest revenues ever recorded in the history of the industry.

I applaud this record growth in large part because many Indian tribes use gaming revenues to fund economic development activities on reservations and to provide government services to their people, including health services, early education programs, and language and cultural preservation activities.

Clearly, gaming has become what Congress intended, a means of promoting tribal economic development, self-sufficiency, and strong tribal governments. Yet, decisions by the Secretary of the Interior to take land into trust for gaming purposes pursuant to the legal standards set forth in Federal law, including the Indian Reorganization Act and IGRA, have raised difficult and contentious issues, especially when those lands are located off-reservation. The result has, unfortunately, pitted tribes with existing gaming operations against their neighbors, both Indians and non-Indian.

But it is my strong belief that the existing statutory and regulatory framework, the IGRA, its implementing regulations at 25 CFR part 292, and the land in trust regulations at 25 CFR part 151 contain adequate safeguards to ensure that the Secretary's decision to allow off-reservation gaming are made wisely, prudently, and in full consideration of local communities that are impacted by those activities.

The IGRA, unlike any other Federal law, and at significant expense to tribal sovereignty, grants a State's Governor veto power over the Secretary of the Interior's two-part determination to authorize off-reservation gaming.

In a legal memorandum issued during the Bush administration, counselors to the Secretary of the Interior opined that the veto power potentially limits the market opportunities of sovereign Indian tribes, but determined that providing States with authority to deny tribes access to lands for gaming was a critical check on the Secretary's discretion under the law. This delicate balance of Federal, State, and tribal power is what makes IGRA an exceptional Federal law.

That said, with the ever-increasing success of Indian gaming enterprises comes increasing competition over the gaming market share between tribes. Tribes with existing gaming facilities and those tribes who seek to join their ranks have battled publicly over location and authority to conduct gaming activities in the first instance. I am fully aware of these disputes and respect that hard-earned tribal economic self-determination is worth protecting.

But when it is believed that a tribe seeks to encroach on another's market under circumstances that reach beyond IGRA, Congress can step in and be the final arbiter. I, and Ranking Member DeFazio, both supported H.R. 1410, legislation that passed the House by voice vote this week. If enacted into law, H.R. 1410 would prevent any Arizona Tribe from circumventing existing Federal authorities to conducting gaming off reservations. I view that legislation as an example of the safety valve Congress can provide when tribes seek to engage in so-called reservation shopping.

As we hear from our witnesses today, it is important to remember that during the Obama administration alone, 1,300 parcels have been taken into trust for the benefit of Indian tribes. And less than 15 of those parcels are connected to gaming projects. It is also remarkable that, since 1988, under the Republican and Democratic administrations, the Department of the Interior has approved only 15 two-part determination applications, and disapproved 14. Of those 15 successful applications, 5 were vetoed by State Governors and 1 has not yet been acted upon.

I believe these numbers demonstrate that IGRA, part 292, and part 151, work together to provide a system of checks and balances, transparency, and meaningful tribal and local community input in departmental review of tribal gaming applications. I yield back, Mr. Chair.

[The prepared statement of Ms. Hanabusa follows:]

PREPARED STATEMENT OF THE HONORABLE COLLEEN W. HANABUSA, RANKING MEMBER, SUBCOMMITTEE ON INDIAN AND ALASKA NATIVE AFFAIRS

Thank you, Mr. Chairman, for holding today's oversight hearing on the executive branch standards for placing land into trust for gaming purposes.

As this subcommittee is well aware, gaming has provided economic opportunities for Indian tribes that, prior to passage of the Indian Gaming Regulatory Act (IGRA) in 1988, were practically unimaginable. According to the National Indian Gaming Commission, in 2012 alone revenues generated by the Indian gaming industry totaled **$27.9 billion**. These are the highest revenues ever recorded in the history of the industry. I applaud this record growth in large part because many Indian tribes use gaming revenues to fund economic development activities on reservations and to provide government services to their people, including health services, early education programs, and language and cultural preservation activities. Clearly, gaming has become what Congress intended: "a means of promoting tribal economic development, self-sufficiency and strong tribal governments."

Yet, decisions by the Secretary of the Interior to take land into trust for gaming purposes pursuant to the legal standards set forth in Federal law, including the Indian Reorganization Act and the IGRA, have raised difficult and contentious issues—especially when those lands are located off-reservation. The result has unfortunately pitted tribes with existing gaming operations against their neighbors, both Indian and non-Indian.

But it is my strong belief that the existing statutory and regulatory framework—the IGRA, its implementing regulations at 25 CFR part 292 and land-into-trust regulations at 25 CFR part 151—contain adequate safeguards to ensure that the Secretary's decisions to allow off-reservation gaming are made wisely, prudently, and in full consideration of local communities that are impacted by those activities.

The IGRA, unlike any other Federal law and at significant expense to tribal sovereignty, grants a State's Governor **veto power** over the Secretary of the Interior's two-part determination to authorize off-reservation gaming. In a legal memorandum issued during the Bush administration, counselors to the Secretary of the Interior opined that this veto power "potentially limits the market opportunities of sovereign Indian tribes" but determined that providing States with authority to deny tribes access to lands for gaming was a critical check on the Secretary's discretion under the law. This delicate balance of Federal, State, and tribal power is what makes the IGRA an exceptional Federal law.

That said, with the ever increasing success of Indian gaming enterprises, comes increasing competition over gaming market share between tribes. Tribes with existing gaming facilities, and those tribes who seek to join their ranks, have battled publicly over location and authority to conduct gaming activities in the first in-

5

stance. I'm fully aware of these disputes and respect that hard-earned tribal economic self-determination is worth protecting. But when a tribe that seeks to encroach on another's market under circumstances that reach beyond the IGRA, Congress may choose to step in.

I and Ranking Member DeFazio both supported H.R. 1410, legislation that passed the House by voice vote this week. If enacted into law, H.R. 1410 would prevent any Arizona tribe from circumventing existing Federal authorities to conducting gaming off-reservation. I view that legislation as an example of the safety valve Congress can provide when tribes seek to engage in so-called "reservation shopping."

As we hear from our witnesses today, it is important to remember that, during the Obama administration alone, **1,300** parcels have been taken into trust for the benefit of Indian tribes, and less than **15** of those parcels are connected to gaming projects. It is also remarkable that, since 1988, under Republican and Democratic administrations, the Department of the Interior has **approved** only 15, 2 part determination applications, and **disapproved** 14. Of these 15 successful applications, 5 were vetoed by the States' Governors and one has not been acted upon yet.

I believe these numbers demonstrate that the IGRA, part 292 and part 151 work together to provide a system of checks and balances, transparency and meaningful tribal and local community input in Departmental review of tribal gaming applications. I yield back.

———

Mr. YOUNG. I thank the good lady. We now have one witness on the first panel. Mr. Washburn is there as the Assistant Secretary of Indian Affairs, U.S. Department of the Interior.

Mr. Washburn, thank you. And I won't read you the rules, but you have 5 minutes or as long as you wish to take, as long as you are not filibustering. So go right ahead, Kevin, go right ahead.

[Laughter.]

STATEMENT OF KEVIN K. WASHBURN, ASSISTANT SECRETARY FOR INDIAN AFFAIRS, U.S. DEPARTMENT OF THE INTERIOR

Mr. WASHBURN. Chairman Young, thank you so much. Ranking Member Hanabusa and members of the committee, it is an honor to be here to talk about Ronald Reagan's, Don Young's and Mo Udall's Indian Gaming Regulatory Act.

In IGRA, Congress gave the power to the Secretary to allow certain off-reservation gaming to occur on lands taken into trust after October 17, 1988. Like Congress, the Secretary has a trust responsibility to American Indian tribes, and so we cannot simply refuse to consider off-reservation gaming applications, nor would we want to do that.

As the Ranking Member Hanabusa has so eloquently stated, it is a very important resource to tribes. Off-reservation gaming has produced great success, often for tribal communities that have very significant economic challenges and very few economic advantages.

That said, most tribes conduct gaming on land that is within their reservations. And it is very rare for us to use the authority provided in IGRA to take land into trust off the reservation for Indian gaming.

In any given case, these tend to be very difficult and very controversial decisions. I come to each one, frankly, with a healthy skepticism because I know that it needs to be taken very seriously and carefully justified before we move forward. These decisions take such a long time because we have a lot of process that is involved to make a decision. The process occurs in the field and then here in Washington. The process involves seeking input from the tribes and other communities, such as the counties and the cities nearby, and sometimes the State.

The process is lengthy and related to several different substantive areas. We must look at environmental considerations. We must consider substantive decisions regarding not just the gaming, but historical connections to the land, cultural values, economic and other considerations. We also have to make substantive decisions about the land itself, the land to be taken into trust. So, the process is very rigorous, and uses a lot of different factors, an extensive list of factors, as you can see from my written testimony.

The process also costs tribes hundreds of thousands of dollars, even when the final outcome is negative. For the tribe that has run the gauntlet successfully, they must obtain not only an approval from the Department of the Interior, but, in many cases, approval by the Governor of the State in which the land is located. In other words, the State has a veto over any off-reservation land-into-trust gaming.

It routinely takes several years for a tribe to get any land into trust for gaming. It tends to be much longer for off-reservation lands. And, Chairman, I understand it seems like a rubber stamp to some people, but it is a very slow rubber stamp, if it is a rubber stamp. It takes us a very, very, very long time to make these decisions. And whether it happens too quickly or too slowly depends on your perspective. Tribes interested in having lands taken into trust for gaming tend to complain over and over that the process takes way too long. People who are opposed tend to complain that it moves too fast, even when it does take years.

Our job at Interior is to listen to the opinions of all the relevant constituencies, and try to make an informed decision, a decision that has been given to us by Congress to make. We do the best we can. We make these decisions in a context in which we also have to make decisions about housing, about law enforcement, about social services, about fire suppression, about dam maintenance. Lately we have been having lots of floods and fires. Courts and justice systems, we have to deal with corrections systems, we have to deal with schools and education, which are very important. Agricultural and irrigation systems, and highways and roads, and many other issues.

And so off-reservation gaming is one of the very many things that we think that are important in Indian Country. But we are happy to hear your thoughts on this subject, and happy to be here to answer any questions. Thank you, Chairman.

[The prepared statement of Mr. Washburn follows:]

PREPARED STATEMENT OF KEVIN K. WASHBURN, ASSISTANT SECRETARY FOR INDIAN AFFAIRS, U.S. DEPARTMENT OF THE INTERIOR

Good afternoon Chairman Young, Ranking Member Hanabusa, and members of the subcommittee. My name is Kevin Washburn, and I am the Assistant Secretary for Indian Affairs at the Department of the Interior (Department). Thank you for the opportunity to provide the Department's views at this oversight hearing on the executive branch's standards for land-in-trust decisions for gaming purposes.

BACKGROUND AND OVERVIEW OF FEDERAL POLICIES RELATING TO TRIBAL LANDS

As this committee is well aware, in 1887 Congress passed the ill-fated General Allotment Act. More than a century later, tribes continue to feel the effects of this repudiated and devastating policy that divided tribal lands, allotted parcels to individual tribal members and provided for the public sale of any surplus tribal lands remaining after allotment. The General Allotment Act resulted in the loss of approximately two-thirds of the tribal land base, set in motion the current fractionation problem of individual trust allotments and established the "checkerboard" pattern of ownership on many Indian reservations. In less than 50 years, tribal ownership of tribal lands plummeted from 130 million acres to 49 million acres with tribes losing 80 percent of the value of their lands.

In 1934, Congress took action to reverse the destructive assimilation policies of the General Allotment Act, enacting the Indian Reorganization Act (IRA) to promote tribal self-determination and economic development. The Indian Reorganization Act expressly discontinued the allotment of Indian lands and permanently continued the trust status of those lands retained by tribal members. In order to promote tribal self-determination and economic development, Congress authorized the Secretary to place lands in trust for Indian tribes. This fundamental component remains the primary means by which the Department implements the IRA's "overriding purpose" of ensuring that "Indian tribes would be able to assume a greater degree of self-government, both politically and economically." *Morton* v. *Mancari,* 417 U.S. 535, 542 (1974). Nearly 80 years later, self-determination and self-governance have proven to be the right Federal policy. Lands held in trust for tribes continue to fall woefully short of the 130 million acres owned by tribes in 1887, despite the administration's efforts to prioritize fee-to-trust acquisitions.

FEE-TO-TRUST LAND ACQUISITION FOR GAMING PURPOSES

The Department's process for acquiring land in trust for tribes is rigorous. Before any land will be placed into trust, regardless of the purposes for which it will be used, the applicant tribe must satisfy the requirements set forth at 25 CFR part 151 (part 151). Pursuant to part 151, the Department considers the following factors before accepting any land into trust: the tribe's need for the land; the purpose for which the land will be used; the statutory authority to accept the land in trust; jurisdictional and land use concerns; the Bureau of Indian Affairs' ability to manage the land; and compliance with all necessary environmental laws. 25 CFR § 151.10. Compliance with all necessary environmental laws includes compliance with the National Environmental Policy Act (NEPA). NEPA is used as the vehicle for identifying and addressing the various Federal, tribal, State, and local environmental requirements necessary for accepting the land into trust. NEPA requires preparation of an Environmental Assessment or Environmental Impact Statement, both of which provide opportunities for State, local and public comment on the potential impacts of placing the land into trust. Importantly, the Department also considers the impact that the acquisition will have on the State and local governments with regulatory jurisdiction over the land resulting from removal of the land from the tax rolls, and any jurisdictional problems and potential conflicts of land use.

Off-reservation acquisitions must meet a heightened standard. Along with the requirements for tribal trust acquisitions under § 151.10, the Department considers additional factors under § 151.11 relating to the location of the land relative to State boundaries; the distance of the land from the tribe's reservation; the tribe's business plan; and concerns from State and local governments. The Department gives "greater scrutiny to the tribe's justification of anticipated benefits from the acquisition . . . [and] greater weight to the concerns raised" by the local community the farther the proposed acquisition is from the tribe's reservation. Further, the Department notifies State and local governments having regulatory jurisdiction over the land at issue and requests their comments concerning potential impacts on regulatory jurisdiction, real property taxes and special assessments.

There is a misperception that the Department commonly accepts off-reservation land into trust for gaming purposes. However, the facts show that of the 1,300 trust acquisitions since 2008, fewer than 15 were for gaming purposes and even fewer were for off-reservation gaming purposes. There are presently four applications pending that were submitted by tribes seeking to conduct gaming on lands contiguous to their reservations and nine applications pending for gaming on off-reservation land acquired in trust after the enactment of IGRA.

As you know, section 20 of the Indian Gaming Regulatory Act (IGRA) allows for gaming on off-reservation lands acquired in trust after IGRA's enactment on October 17, 1988 only in very limited instances. There are a few limited and narrow statutory exceptions that operate to provide equal footing for tribes that would otherwise be disadvantaged. These include: the initial reservation of an Indian tribe acknowledged by the Secretary under the Federal acknowledgment process, restored lands for tribes restored after termination, and lands acquired in settlement of a land claim. In other cases, off-reservation trust lands are eligible for gaming only if the tribe satisfies the rigorous standards set forth in Departmental regulations at subpart C of 25 CFR part 292, and generally known as the "Secretarial Determination" or "two-part determination." These regulations, promulgated by the previous administration, require a tribe to demonstrate that the proposed off-reservation gaming establishment is in the best interest of the tribe, taking into account a wide range of information, including information regarding:

- Projected tribal income and employment;
- Projected benefits to the tribe and its members from projected income;
- Possible adverse impacts on the tribe and its members and plans of addressing such impacts; and
- Distance of the land from the location where the tribe maintains core governmental functions.

The tribe must also demonstrate that the proposed gaming facility will not be detrimental to the surrounding community. The applicant must provide information on the following:

- Anticipated impacts on the social structure, infrastructure, services, housing, community character and land use patterns of the surrounding community;
- Anticipated impacts on the economic development, income and employment of the surrounding community; and
- If any nearby tribe has a significant historical connection to the land, the impact on that tribe's traditional cultural connection to the land.

Further, the Department consults with State and local officials, including officials of nearby tribes, regarding the application. The Department then evaluates all the information. Even if the Department concludes that the gaming establishment is in the best interest of the applicant tribe and not detrimental to the surrounding community, the Governor of the State retains the ultimate authority to veto any gaming on the parcel. In the 25 years since the passage of IGRA, only eight times has a Governor concurred in a positive two-part Secretarial determination made pursuant to section 20(b)(1)(A) of IGRA.

It is important to note that the public, State, and local governments, and other tribal governments, have many opportunities to participate throughout the process. As noted above, prior to deciding whether to place the off-reservation land into trust, the Department seeks comment from State and local governments; the public and local governments may also provide input during the NEPA process. Moreover, before off-reservation land can be found eligible for gaming through the two-part determination process, the Department requests additional comments from nearby tribal, State and local governments. In most cases, tribes and local governments enter into agreements to address impacts of placing land into trust for gaming, often compensating local governments for impacts.

In sum, the Department's review of land in trust applications—regardless of location or the activity that is proposed for the land to be acquired—is rigorous and considers the concerns of all stakeholders, including the applicant tribe as well as potentially impacted State, local and tribal governments and the public at large.

This concludes my prepared statement. I am happy to answer any questions the subcommittee may have concerning land-into-trust applications for gaming.

QUESTIONS SUBMITTED FOR THE RECORD TO KEVIN K. WASHBURN

QUESTIONS SUBMITTED FOR THE RECORD BY THE HONORABLE PETER A. DEFAZIO

Question. If a tribe already has one casino in their aboriginal territory, should they be allowed to place land into trust outside their aboriginal territory—and in another tribe's aboriginal territory—to open a second casino?

Answer. The Department follows all statutory and regulatory requirements when making determinations for tribal applications to acquire land in trust for gaming. The Indian Reorganization Act (IRA) does not impose aboriginal territory limitations on trust land acquisitions. The Indian Gaming Regulatory Act (IGRA) also does not limit the number of casinos a tribe may have, nor does it limit the locations where those facilities may be located. Section 20 of IGRA prohibits tribes from using land acquired in trust after October 17, 1988 for gaming purposes unless the land meets one of the statutory exceptions.

The Department's regulations at 25 CFR part 292 require that tribes seeking to conduct gaming on off-reservation sites pursuant to the "Secretarial determination," or "two-part" exception, include information regarding the distance of the land from the location of the tribe's government headquarters and its core governmental functions. The regulations also require that tribes include evidence of significant historical connections to the land, if any. *See* 25 CFR §§ 292.16–292.18. Although Congress did not explicitly require these factors to be considered in IGRA, they are considered in the Department's Secretarial determination.

Question. If a tribe already has a casino, but wants an additional casino in a bigger market, how does your agency view that proposal if the desired new market is not in that tribe's aboriginal territory?

Answer. As noted in the response to the previous question, the Department follows all statutory and regulatory requirements when making determinations for tribal applications to acquire land in trust for gaming. Neither the IRA nor IGRA impose aboriginal territory limitations on off-reservation gaming sites. The regulations at 25 CFR part 292 provide specific criteria that the Department follows when making determinations on tribal applications to take land into trust for gaming. Part 292 requires tribes to include evidence of significant historical connections to the land, if any. The criteria in part 292 are considered in the Department's final two-part determinations regarding land acquisitions for gaming.

Question. There is no authority under the Indian Reorganization Act for placing lands into trust for gaming after 1988, correct? So any new trust land request for gaming cannot be authorized under the IRA?

Answer. The IRA places no temporal limitations on the Secretary's discretion for placing land into trust for gaming or other purposes. The IGRA does, however, in certain circumstances prohibit gaming on trust lands acquired after October 17, 1988, unless the land meets certain statutory exceptions enumerated in section 20 of IGRA.

QUESTION SUBMITTED FOR THE RECORD BY THE HONORABLE PAUL A. GOSAR

SECOND AMENDMENT BUSINESS LEASE BETWEEN THE PIMA CENTER AND MEMBERS OF THE SALT RIVER PIMA—MARICOPA INDIAN COMMUNITY

Question. On May 23, my Arizona colleague Congressman David Schweikert sent a letter to Assistant Secretary Washburn asking him to facilitate conversations between the BIA Western Regional Office and the PIMA Center management to ensure the timely agreement and completion of a Second Amendment Business Lease between the PIMA Center and Members of the Salt River Pima—Maricopa Indian Community.

In August, he finally received a response from the BIA Western Regional Office. Despite assurances from the BIA Western Regional Office that they were working diligently to complete the approval process, it is my understanding that the agreement still has not been completed.

This lease agreement has approval from the Tribal Council of Salt River Pima—Maricopa Indian Community and an overwhelming majority of the property's landowners. What is holding up the completion of this agreement? Is there some legal issue preventing final approval?

Answer. The Second Amendment that was the subject of Congressman Schweikert's inquiry has now effectively been withdrawn, and replaced by a Revised Second Amendment that is considered "deemed approved" by BIA, under applicable regulations. It is expected that a new Third Amendment will soon be submitted to BIA's Western Regional Office ("WRO"), seeking at least a partial 20-year extension of the maximum lease term (a broad extension that provision having been removed from the Revised Second Amendment, in order to expedite its approval).

As indicated in the August 5, 2013, interim response to Congressman Schweikert, WRO has taken the position that the rent payable under the lease should be increased during any broad extension period. At a September 12, 2013, landowners meeting, the reasons for this position were discussed, along with relevant regulations and options as to how and when such increases might be effected. A final response was provided (by copy of a November 4, 2013, letter responding to an earlier, near-identical inquiry from Senator Flake), and a follow-up meeting to discuss possible future amendments with the parties is scheduled for December 11, 2013.

QUESTION SUBMITTED FOR THE RECORD BY THE HONORABLE MARKWAYNE MULLIN

Question. In general, I want to know what BIA's position is on tribes taking advantage of lucrative markets in other tribes' backyards where they do not have an aboriginal footprint.

Would your agency's rules allow a tribe from say California to acquire land for gaming in Oklahoma?

Answer. The Department follows all statutory and regulatory requirements when making determinations for tribal applications to acquire land in trust for gaming. Neither the IRA nor IGRA impose aboriginal territory limitations on off-reservation gaming sites. The Department's regulations at 25 CFR part 292 require consideration of many factors before making a determination on an off-reservation gaming application. Those factors include such things as the distance of the proposed gaming site from the applicant tribe's government headquarters, the existence of the applicant tribe's significant historical connection to the proposed gaming site, if any, and the possible adverse impacts on the applicant tribe and its members and plans for addressing those impacts. *See* 25 CFR § 292.17(f), (g) and (i).

QUESTIONS SUBMITTED FOR THE RECORD BY THE HONORABLE GWEN MOORE, A REPRESENTATIVE IN CONGRESS FROM THE STATE OF WISCONSIN

PREVENTING RESERVATION SHOPPING

Question. The Department of Interior adopted regulations on Gaming on After Acquired Lands in 2008, 25 CFR part 292, which retain the Secretary's broad discretion to approve the off-reservation or Secretarial Determination exception. As you know, many Members of Congress and others believe that "reservation shopping" is a big problem for Indian gaming because it undermines the credibility of Indian gaming as governmental gaming and it makes tribes look like they are simply commercial casino developers. As I see it, there are two main hallmarks of "reservation shopping"—when a tribe seeks to go a long distance from its homeland or existing Indian lands, and when a tribe chooses a casino site for obviously commercial or market considerations. There are two important protections against "reservation shopping" in IGRA and the part 292 regulations. The first is to require that the applicant tribe has a significant historic connection to the land in question. The second is to require that the casino not detrimentally impact the surrounding community. On August 23, 2013, the Assistant Secretary issued a Secretarial Determination for a casino on the Wisconsin-Illinois border, located 160 miles from the Menominee Reservation in northern Wisconsin, even though the Menominee Tribe already has a successful casino hotel on its reservation and it has more tribal land than any other tribe in the region. Now, I am sure that you believe this will be good for the Menominee Tribe, but it appears to many that this decision will open the floodgates for reservation shopping across the country. Doesn't this decision prove to those in Congress who oppose reservation shopping that we need legislation to crack down on these far flung casino applications?

Answer. The IGRA specifies a two-part test in reviewing applications to acquire off-reservation land in trust for gaming. This Secretarial Determination, or two-part determination, permits a tribe to conduct gaming on lands acquired in trust after October 17, 1988, if the Secretary determines (1) that gaming on the land would be in the best interest of the tribe and its members, and (2) not detrimental to the surrounding community. Gaming may occur only if the Governor of the State in which the land is located concurs with the Secretary's determination.

In the 25 years since the enactment of IGRA, the Secretary has made 14 two-part determinations and Governors have exercised their veto power to preclude gaming in 5 of those. The applications are rare and considered on a case-by-case basis. Most of the decisions that were approved by Governors were relatively close to the tribe's existing reservation, with the exception of the Forest County Potawatomi Community which was 210 miles from its reservation, and the Menominee, which was 160 miles from its reservation. The Department's recent Secretarial Determination for Menominee favorably referenced the Forest County determination. Unlike the Forest County application, the Menominee application analyzed information from a detailed Environmental Impact Statement and a voluminous record. Because IGRA gives the Governor authority to decline to concur with a positive two-part determination, the Department does not believe additional legislation is required.

SIGNIFICANT HISTORIC CONNECTION

Question. As you know, most Indian tribes and national and regional Indian organizations are concerned that the Secretary will approve casinos for one tribe in the historic or aboriginal lands of another tribe. I'm sure you will acknowledge that the concern of tribes over the protection of their historic lands against encroachment by other tribes is widely shared in Indian country. In your Secretarial Determination on the Kenosha Casino, you state that an applicant tribe is not required to establish a "significant historic connection" to the land in order for the Secretary to conclude that a proposed casino would be in the best interest of the tribe. However, isn't it also true that Interior's Regulations require every applicant tribe to submit evidence of their historic connection to the area, if they have any? In the case of Kenosha, however, you chose not to decide whether the Menominee Tribe had a significant historic connection as they claim in their application. You chose to do this, I presume, because it is clear that the Menominee Tribe does not have a significant historic connection and the tribe did not submit evidence of actual occupation, villages or burial sites or any treaty history over the Kenosha area as your regulations require. Instead the tribe relied on oral history which your prior decisions have clearly held is not adequate. Don't you agree that the Potawatomi Nation does have a significant historic connection to Kenosha and that Potawatomi established that fact in its submission to the BIA with treaties, the decisions of the Indian Claims Commission, and evidence of villages and burial sites within Kenosha County? So, given the Potawatomi Nation's overwhelming evidence of a significant historic connection to the land, wouldn't it have been more appropriate for the Secretarial Determination to either clearly state that Menominee has no significant historic connection to the land or to apply the required definition of "significant historic connection" to this evidence rather than simply side-step the issue? It looks to me that the Secretary has decided to ignore the historic connection of tribes to their land. Doesn't this mean "reservation shopping" is allowed, if not encouraged?

Answer. In IGRA Congress did not require an analysis of a significant historical connection. However, the Department's regulations at 25 CFR part 292 incorporate such an analysis into decisionmaking in certain cases. The discussion in the Menominee Secretarial Determination that an applicant tribe is not required to establish a "significant historical connection" for the two-part determination clarifies the regulatory process, but is not an analysis of the tribe's submission. In a two-part determination, evidence of a significant historical connection is relevant but not determinative. The Department does not encourage off-reservation gaming applications. Indeed, they are difficult and time consuming, but the law gives the Department the responsibility to consider them and make difficult decisions.

The Potawatomi Nation has broad historical and contemporary connections throughout the Midwest and in Kansas and Oklahoma. In this case, the Department was not considering an application by any of the bands of the Potawatomi Nation, but only of the Menominee Tribe. The Menominee Tribe submitted evidence of a significant historical connection which the Department examined. The evidence included documents indicating that the Menominee Tribe was an original inhabitant of the area around Kenosha. While the regulations state that a significant historical connection is not required to make a determination that the project would be in the best interest of the tribe, the Department reviewed the tribal history, academic historical research, maps, and other evidence. The decision specifically cites historical documentation submitted by the Menominee Tribe which includes: a written Overview of the Menominee History by the Menominee Indian Tribe; The Mero Complex and the Menominee Tribe: Prospects for a Territorial Ethnicity by David Overstreet, Maps of the Mero Complex and the historic range of the Menominee and The Traditional Relationship of the Menominee Indian Tribe of Wisconsin to the city of Kenosha and the Southeastern Region of Menominee Country, by David R.M. Beck. The Department's decision was also based on historical information in the final Environmental Impact Statement.

IGNORING EVIDENCE OF DETRIMENTAL IMPACT

Question. I am concerned that the BIA does not give fair consideration to the concerns of nearby Indian tribes and surrounding communities in applying the requirements for a Secretarial Determination. I am told that the BIA has never decided that there is a detrimental impact on the surrounding community or a nearby Indian tribe from any off reservation gaming application. Is that correct? Isn't it reasonable for me to conclude therefore, that the BIA simply does not support the provision of IGRA which requires the Secretary to evaluate impact on the surrounding community, because you always conclude there is no detrimental impact. I am sure you disagree, but let me give you an example from Illinois. Over 25 separate letters from Illinois State, local and Federal officials expressing concern over the environmental, economic, and social impacts of the proposed Kenosha Casino on the surrounding community within Illinois were submitted to the BIA. Local Illinois officials held their own public hearing on the Kenosha Casino, they have testified before this committee, and they have expressed their concern to all levels of the BIA over the past 8 years. You can imagine the surprise of these Illinois officials when your August 23, 2013 Secretarial Determination stated, at 45, fn. 322 "Lake County and Milwaukee County responded after the comment period had run and were therefore not considered." In the Kenosha Secretarial Determination, you simply chose to avoid the evidence of detrimental impact in Illinois by applying a procedural device. The BIA apparently claims it is not obligated to evaluate the obvious detrimental impact on Illinois, despite the fact that the record is undisputed that there is detrimental impact. Don't you understand, then, why many say that the Assistant Secretary of Indian Affairs simply is not fairly applying this provision of the law by ignoring detrimental impacts? This same result occurred in the City and County of Milwaukee where local officials and Congresswoman Moore have tried for many years to insure that the detrimental impacts on the City and County of Milwaukee are properly considered. Isn't it the case that the BIA simply uses bureaucratic devices to avoid giving fair consideration to the detrimental impact once it decides it should grant an application?

Answer. As noted in a previous response, the Department is required by section 20 of IGRA to analyze whether a proposed project would be detrimental to the surrounding community. The Department's regulations implementing Section 20 at 25 CFR Part 292 identify the criteria the Secretary must analyze in order to make such a determination. The Department must follow the requirements in the law and these regulations. The Department considered the views of the City and County of Milwaukee in making its determination. As discussed in the Secretarial Determination, both the City and County of Milwaukee are located within 25 miles of the proposed gaming facility and, thus, the Department was required to consult with them and consider their views. The County and the City presented evidence that the proposed gaming facility in Kenosha would compete with another gaming facility in Milwaukee. Economic analysis and market analysis suggests that the proposed gaming facility would lead to a competitive impact that might have limited short term economic impacts in their respective communities but market-based competition is not prohibited by the Indian Gaming Regulatory Act. *See Sokaogon Chippewa Community* v. *Babbitt,* 214 F.3d 941, 947 (7th Cir. 2000).

The determination considered the comments of the local communities at pages 45 through 51 of the decision. Of the 180 comment letters sent out, only Lake County and Milwaukee County failed to submit comments by the deadline in the letter. The two-part determination considered the concerns of Milwaukee County along with the comments of Milwaukee City. On April 30, 2012, the Regional Director responded to the Milwaukee County's letter dated March 28, 2012, requesting to participate in the Consultation Notice process. In its response, the Regional Director explained that his office sent two Consultation Notices to Milwaukee County, and received signed returned receipt cards for both of the Consultation Notices, and that, based on the record the comment time period for Milwaukee County had expired. On June 18, 2012, Milwaukee County provided comments. Because Milwaukee County alleged it had not received any of the consultation letters, the Regional Director included the comments in the record and shared the comments with the Menominee Tribe which responded to the comments by letter dated June 26, 2012.

Lake County, Illinois, is located within 25 miles of the proposed gaming facility, and the Department was required to consult with this county government. The County failed to respond to the Department's consultation letter in the time allotted by our regulations. Therefore the Department did not consider the views of Lake County, Illinois, in making its determination. The Department is bound by the timeframes specified in the regulations and believes that fairness requires treating commentators the same with regard to these important procedural rules.

Detrimental impacts to local communities are addressed in the Environmental Impact Statement, along with measures to mitigate those impacts. Additionally, the local communities where the project is located have entered into intergovernmental agreements with the Menominee Tribe to further mitigate possible adverse impacts. To date, we have found no detrimental impact to the surrounding community after the mitigation measures required by the Environmental Impact Statement are considered.

DOI AUTHORIZES "RESERVATION SHOPPING"

Question. So, on August 23, 2013, the Assistant Secretary issued a Secretarial Determination for a casino on the Wisconsin-Illinois border, located 160 miles from the Menominee Reservation in northern Wisconsin, even though the Menominee Tribe already has a successful casino hotel on its reservation and it has more tribal land than any other tribe in the region. This approval was issued without analyzing the comments submitted by the members of the surrounding community, Milwaukee County or Lake County, Illinois, that will experience extensive detrimental impacts if the Kenosha Casino is opened and without finding that the Menominee have a significant historic connection to the Kenosha land. Now, I am sure that you believe this will be good for the Menominee Tribe, but how does ignoring the requirements of IGRA and your own part 292 regulations not lead to "reservation shopping" throughout the United States? Doesn't this prove to those in Congress who oppose reservation shopping that we need legislation to crack down on these far flung casino applications?

13

Answer. As discussed in the responses to the previous questions, the IGRA does not limit the locations where gaming facilities may be located and, thus, the Department does not believe that off-reservation land taken into trust is a violation of IGRA. In addition, State Governors have authority under IGRA to decline to concur with the Department's positive two-part determination. The previous gaming acquisition for the Forest County Potawatomi Community provides precedent in Wisconsin for the Menominee's application. The Department's Secretarial Determination, which can be found at *www.indianaffairs.gov/cs/groups/public/documents/text/idc1-022944.pdf,* contains a lengthy, detailed discussion addressing many of the concerns of the local communities.

———

Mr. YOUNG. Thank you, Kevin. Madam.

Ms. HANABUSA. Thank you. It is so nice to know that this is the Ronald Reagan, Don Young, and Mo Udall bill.

[Laughter.]

Ms. HANABUSA. With that——

Mr. YOUNG. It was a gamble.

Ms. HANABUSA. It was a gamble. You are really up today.

Mr. Washburn, we have a process that takes place before final regulations are issued. The process has, of course, many requirements, including receiving and considering public comments. The rule defining surrounding community imposes a 25-mile radius for input from local governments and nearby Indian tribes. The Department has addressed the comments and concerns with the rule, but ultimately found that the rule is reasonable, useful, consistent throughout the regulations, and provide uniformity to all parties.

What I would like you to answer are two points. One is did the Obama administration promulgate the 25-mile rule? And, second, are proposals such as either increasing, decreasing, doing away with the radius, desirable? And can a tribe that is beyond the 25-mile radius petition for a consultation or being part of the process?

Mr. WASHBURN. Thank you, Madam Ranking Member. No, these rules were not promulgated by the Obama administration. These rules were promulgated in May 20, 2008, by the George W. Bush administration, when Secretary Kempthorne was the Secretary of the Interior. And we have not changed them. We have looked at them and continued to follow them.

And, yes, the second question is yes. A tribe that is beyond the 25-mile limit can petition to be a cooperating agency or to participate in the discussion about the off-reservation gaming and be heard. And just to be fair, I tend to give audience to any tribal leader that ever wants to meet with me, so I, frankly, hear from tribes that are even beyond the 25-mile limit, and I don't turn them away.

Ms. HANABUSA. How about the 25-mile limit itself? I have heard discussions of either expanding it, reducing it, or doing away with it completely. Do you have an opinion about whether 25 miles is a good radius, or should it change?

Mr. WASHBURN. Thank you, Madam Ranking Member. You know, any amount of miles would ultimately be arbitrary. And so we have got to draw a limit somewhere. And so, I do know that changing that would take—it always takes at least 2 years to do any regulatory change. And given the fact that we are worried about our schools and our dams and our forest fires and other things, it is not something that we have chosen to spend time on, amending our regulations.

Because, frankly, if we did 30 miles or we did 50 miles or we did 10 miles, there would be people that had a problem with that, too. So, ultimately, anything is arbitrary. But 25 miles seems to work. It certainly gets a wide response from people that are interested in the gaming project.

Ms. HANABUSA. One of the things that I found to be interesting was what I call the Governor's veto power under IGRA, or under the circumstances we are discussing here. And also, am I correct in the statistic or the fact that, since then, the Governor has concurred only eight times with any application on the two-part determination under section 20? And it seems like any kind of allegation about a tribe reservation shopping should be curbed by that. So can you explain to me how that works and what criteria, if any, a Governor is required to apply when he or she determines to veto?

Mr. WASHBURN. Yes, Ranking Member Hanabusa. That is sort of a political judgment by the Governor of the State, and the Governor does have that ability to veto. And the Governor can use the factors that they wish, to guide that political determination. And it seems a sensible type of approach, because the Governor obviously knows the community even better than we do, sitting here in Washington. And so I think that is an effective check on this power that Congress has given to the Secretary.

And you are right, I guess the majority of the time, the Governors have approved, but on many occasions they have declined to approve. So it is a real check. We don't get a rubber stamp from a Governor on an off-reservation land-into-trust application.

Ms. HANABUSA. Do you know how many off-reservation gaming applications have been approved since 1988?

Mr. WASHBURN. I believe it is 10, Ranking Member.

Ms. HANABUSA. Thank you. Mr. Chair, I yield back.

Mr. YOUNG. Thank you, ma'am. Mr. LaMalfa.

Mr. LAMALFA. Thank you, Mr. Chairman. A couple, just to start out with here. Thank you for coming here today. I am curious in following up on the Ranking Member's thoughts with the 25 miles or more.

You know, it seems to me kind of naive, with some of the placement here, that a 25-mile limit, especially if we are talking about a fairly flat terrain area, that people aren't going to travel more than 25 miles for their gaming entertainment. And so that the impact should have a wider net, and I don't know how you draw the number, either. But it would have to take into account sometimes people's—maybe an hour's worth of driving would be a limit that you would think of, 50, 60 miles.

So, with some of the placement in northern California we are talking about the BIA, Sacramento, Indian gaming, placing a casino in an area where basically it is right in the path of the customer base and other casinos, how can a study come back and say that there would really be no impact?

And how could, I think that is, I believe that was EES. How can they come up with that determination, that there really would be no economic impact, when it is basically in line of a customer base and other possible gaming facilities in that path?

Mr. WASHBURN. Thank you, Congressman. You know, this is an unusual area, where the government has a significant role in sort of making decisions about how a market is going to work. And the market for gaming, you know, is a distinct market. Gaming is a type of entertainment that lots of people seek out. And certainly, a new gaming operation may very well have effects on existing gaming operations. And I suspect that they may sometimes have an effect on gaming operations that are more than 25 miles away, as you suggest.

I am not sure why the administration, the Bush administration, ultimately settled on 25 miles. I know that they considered 10 miles and they considered 50 miles as possible alternatives, but it is what they ultimately selected and it is sort of what we have been handed. And so, again——

Mr. LaMALFA. You talked about being a regulatory change and taking 2 years. Now, you know, we see executive orders, at the wave of the wand, things change overnight. Why couldn't we have a quicker process? I know there are a lot of things to do. You mentioned, you know, forestry issues, things like that. But, I mean, why couldn't it be done in a short period of time, especially since it appears not to be a just situation?

And, of course, you could take into account, too, maybe you have different geographical factors, too. Maybe when you are talking about a flat valley area you could cast a wider net. And maybe if it is a mountainous area you would have some kind of different criteria, where travel is not quite as conducive. Why can't we shorten the window on relooking at that regulation?

Mr. WASHBURN. Well, Congressman, keep in mind that even a tribe that is outside the 25 miles nevertheless can petition to have their voice heard to be consulted on that gaming operation. So even if they are outside of 25 miles, they can raise their hand and say, "We think this is going to affect us, and we would like to be heard, too." So, even the regulation as it exists allows tribes that are outside the 25-mile area to be heard.

As to doing things quickly, if we were inclined to change it, the Administrative Procedures Act requires us to go through notice-and-comment rulemaking. And, frankly, notice-and-comment rulemaking is a good way to make decisions because it allows people that are interested in the question to be heard. And we have to follow the APA. And it just inevitably seems to take a long time. We have——

Mr. LaMALFA. Well, you know, I appreciate they can raise their hand and say, "We would like to be consulted," but in the case of Colusa in northern California, they were asked to prove a detrimental effect to them. It wasn't just, "Hey, we would like to be heard;" they actually had to provide their own information and prove this in the process, and that doesn't seem like it is in that spirit of being heard and being taken into account. How would you address that?

Mr. WASHBURN. Well, I mean we trust them to have the best judgment about whether it is going to harm them than some third party that is not them. I mean I would think that they would be the ones most interested, they are the ones that have the incentive to show the detriment. And so they seem to be the right people to ask to show that. In that case, you know, it seems to make sense to put the burden of proof on the people saying that it is true to go ahead and make the case. And we would certainly listen if they did.

Mr. LaMalfa. Certainly, well a lot of times it is third parties that are the ones that are trusted because of the self-interest type of thing. So it would seem like that would come from BIA and others within the organization to take that into account.

Mr. Chairman, I will yield back. Thank you.

Mr. Young. Thank you. And we will have a second round, if we wish to do so.

Mr. Washburn, who does these studies for you? The Department doesn't do it.

Mr. Washburn. Generally not the Department. Generally our interested parties submit studies to us. And sometimes they submit economic studies, they submit other kind of studies, historical studies. And they often come in from both the people proposing the application and those who are opposed to it, as well.

Mr. Young. Well, what I am leading up to, you don't have the expertise or something to really look at this in a broad picture, instead of someone that is hired? The guys hired on both sides, they are like lawyers you hire.

Mr. Washburn. Right.

Mr. Young. So, you know, I excuse myself to the lawyers; no, I don't.

[Laughter.]

Mr. Young. But reality is, how do you base your decision on Mr. Mullin's presentation. I make a presentation, and you really don't know anything about the subject, how do you do that?

Mr. Washburn. Chairman, you are the one that gave us this authority, so we use that wisdom that you assumed that we must have——

Mr. Young. But you do not have.

[Laughter.]

Mr. Young. And so, what I am leading up to the committee, there may be time and should be time to review this issue. Because I am not blaming Mr. Washburn for being involved in this at all. I am just saying that there is something wrong here that wasn't meant: distance, economic impact, you know, the whole gamut.

Twenty-five miles doesn't mean anything to me, but I am deeply concerned about an existing casino in place that has done its job, borrowed the money, set up the structure, knows what has to be taken in, and then you have another casino 180 miles away, jumps over the mountains, already has their own, over the mountains, and establishes or looks for lands in trust to build a casino. That just doesn't make sense to me.

Anyway, Mr. Ruiz, you are up next.

Dr. Ruiz. Thank you, Mr. Chairman. I also want to thank you, Assistant Secretary Washburn, for your service to our country and your service to Indian Country. And I want to commend Larry and Darren for the good work that you are doing on behalf of the tribes throughout our country.

I also want to say thank you, Doctor, for always having an open-door policy, and never turning away any tribe who wants audience from you. And I believe that is very important, that you continue to listen to every tribe that comes your way. And I appreciate the serious consideration that you are making to this very controversial issue of off-reservation gaming, and listening to the issues that most people have against off-reservation gaming.

I also want to recognize you guys' hard work. As Ranking Member Hanabusa mentioned, those statistics, you guys are actually turning out a lot of applications faced with less and less resources on your backs.

My question for you is, can you explain the difference between the on-reservation acquisition versus the more controversial two-part determinants? Not only in the definition, but also the process.

Mr. WASHBURN. Thank you, Doctor, Congressman Ruiz. Yes. Let me explain the difference. Thank you for those compliments, too. The staff here and my staff at the Office of Indian Gaming will appreciate those compliments. They do work very hard, and we do our best under difficult circumstances.

So, the difference between on-reservation land into trust for gaming and off-reservation land into trust for gaming is basically that tribes are considered to have a wide degree of sovereignty on the reservations, on the lands that they already possess, and within their reservations. And so, those are sort of presumptively a place where the tribe can take land into trust and start gaming on it. They aren't terribly controversial, usually. No one seems to argue too much about that.

Off-reservation, however, we go through this much more involved process in which we must show that this, you know, land-into-trust is in the best interest of the tribe and not detrimental to the surrounding community. Plus, the Governor of the State gets to veto that if they don't agree. So, there is, you know, again, a much more involved process. We tend to take much more land into trust within reservations than we do outside of reservations. It is rather unusual for us to go through this elaborate process to take land into trust off reservations.

Dr. RUIZ. So my understanding is when it is contiguous there seems to be a lot more local support and it is less controversial, versus off-reservation, where it is more controversial, and you have to go through a very detailed process.

What is the average length of time that it takes to go with a contiguous on-reservation versus the off-reservation? What are we looking at here?

Mr. WASHBURN. Thank you, Congressman Ruiz. You know, I don't have the exact figures before me. I will tell you that it frequently takes many years for an off-reservation application to go through the process. And contiguous, or on reservation, you know, contiguous tends to be sort of right next to the reservation, but not within the reservation boundaries. But contiguous or on the reservation tends to go more quickly, like you said, because they tend to just have far fewer objections, far fewer people complaining about it because, you know, those are the people who are accustomed to having the tribe exercise sovereignty in that area.

So, I don't know the exact time, but it is much quicker for contiguous, or on-reservation.

Dr. RUIZ. Any example of an on-reservation contiguous land in trust that is different than the off-reservation that you can think of right now?

Mr. WASHBURN. Well, you know, the process, even for contiguous and on-reservation land into trust, it still has to go through the environmental analysis, so NEPA, National Environmental Policy Act. And that process just inevitably takes months and months and months.

So, even those processes take in excess of a year, and often 2 to 3 years, because sometimes issues come up. And then we, for example, have to make sure that we do have a very good survey of that land. Because, after all, we are taking that land into trust, owned by the United States, you know, for the tribe. And so we are very persnickety about the title questions and about the survey questions.

And so, there is still a gauntlet, even for those lands. And that frequently takes 2 to 3 to 4 years, even in that context.

Dr. RUIZ. Well, I appreciate not only your answer, but the word "persnickety." Is that what you used?

[Laughter.]

Dr. RUIZ. I think I am going to have to use that one from now on.

I also want to say, again, thank you for your service to Indian Country, and I look forward to working with you to make sure that these processes are shortened, with your staff, and so that we can work with all the due diligence that we need to make sure we are making the right decisions on these cases.

Mr. WASHBURN. Thank you, Congressman.

Dr. RUIZ. Thank you.

Mr. YOUNG. I thank you gentlemen. Mr. Mullin.

Mr. MULLIN. Thank you. And that is the first time I have seen a doctor actually take time. Mostly they are just in and out real quick. I don't get that.

[Laughter.]

Mr. MULLIN. But I guess, you know, you are a politician now, you have to take more time to talk. I am kidding.

Anyway, hey, as most of you guys know, I am typically pretty passionate when I get up here and get to discuss Indian Country, because of how close to it I come. And, Secretary Washburn, you know you and I have not always seen eye to eye, but I do appreciate your passion and your fight. I disagree with you quite a bit. But then again, I am not doing your job. And I had the opportunity, hindsight is always 20/20.

And right now we are talking about something that is vitally important to Indian Country: gaming. It is what has allowed us to invest back into our people, back into our lands. We have been able to invest into the generations coming behind us. Just yesterday, I had a long conversation with the Cherokee Nation and the wonderful job they have done in investing into their schools and seeing a Tahlequah Sequoyah go from a school that you wouldn't want to go to when I was in high school to a just state-of-the-art facility. And we have been able to do that because of gaming.

But sometimes we have people that want more. And you get stuck in the middle of it. And so, a question that I have for you is when you are looking at the process, your agency is looking at the process, looking at taking land into trust for gaming purposes, specifically what type of input do you receive from the county or local agencies when you are making that consideration?

Mr. WASHBURN. Thank you, Congressman Mullin. And thank you for the kind words. It is good to see a fellow Okie up there.

Mr. MULLIN. I don't know if it was kind or not, but OK.

[Laughter.]

Mr. WASHBURN. Well, you know being Chickasaw, my tribe has done, you know, great, has had real success in great measure, due to gaming. Good leadership, but also gaming.

We look at a lot of different things when we are talking to local communities. We look at the things they care about most. So, you know, for example, there is one that is sort of on our plate, where there is a local military base that the community cares very much about, and we try to take those considerations, you know, we try to consider carefully what they care about.

Ordinarily, in all of the cases, what we think about is infrastructure. Is there infrastructure to manage this gaming operation? Can the roads handle the traffic? We look at whether the water treatment systems are adequate to handle the sewage, and that sort of thing. I mean we go into great depths to figure out whether this community can handle a major economic venture that is going to be——

Mr. MULLIN. Well, even with that, though, a lot of times you see the tribes are willing to invest that themselves.

Mr. WASHBURN. They are. They——

Mr. MULLIN. I mean Chickasaw Nation, and Choctaw, and Cherokee, we have all done that. But do you give, then, the opportunity to veto the land that we are looking to take into trust? That is typically, that is Indian Country, but also on our historical territories.

Mr. WASHBURN. I wouldn't call it quite a veto, but we certainly have to consider the effects on the surrounding community, and determine that it is not detrimental to the surrounding community. And so, you know, often that is sort of a weighing exercise. So it doesn't come out to be a veto.

Frequently, these projects have people who are hotly opposed to it and very much in favor. And we try to figure out, you know, what the right answer is. And it is not easy, because sometimes both of those groups are screaming at us from both sides.

Mr. MULLIN. If I am understanding this correctly, though, if it is on Indian land, it is our trust. That is the authority that the Federal Government has given to us. Is that not correct?

Mr. WASHBURN. That is right. If it is already on Indian lands, that is correct. If it is on an Indian reservation. And, you know——

Mr. MULLIN. Well, Oklahoma doesn't have Indian reservations.

Mr. WASHBURN. Well, in Oklahoma there is a special rule in IGRA. Section 20 of IGRA has just a special rule in Oklahoma, so the lands have to be within the former reservation boundaries that existed in Oklahoma——

Mr. MULLIN. Then why are we seeing in one case, in particular, where we are seeing tribes jump out and go into competition, basically, with another tribe that already has a casino? I know that has already been touched, but if that is the case, then why are we even allowing this to happen? And you know what recent case I am talking about.

Mr. WASHBURN. Yes, Congressman. And you are not going to be pleased, but the matter is in litigation. My lawyers have told me that I can't say too much about those things.

Mr. MULLIN. Then could you please do me a favor and talk to your lawyers and let them get back to us? Because it is a big concern of ours, because in this case I feel like if this is able to happen, then what is going to keep a tribe from California coming into Oklahoma?

And I have run out of time. So please get back to me on that. Mr. Chairman, I yield back.

Mr. YOUNG. Thank you, sir. Mr. Cárdenas.

Mr. CÁRDENAS. Thank you very much, Mr. Chairman. And I am never going to use the word "persnickety."

[Laughter.]

Mr. CÁRDENAS. I was in a hearing once and I used the word "flabbergasted," and to this day my kids don't let me live that down. So good luck.

Mr. YOUNG. You ought to hear some of the words I say.

[Laughter.]

Mr. CÁRDENAS. I wouldn't let my kids listen to me say that.

[Laughter.]

Mr. CÁRDENAS. Well, I would like to focus a bit, Mr. Washburn, on what seems to have developed within the Department when it comes to the interpretations of the latitude of the Department on these decisions under the George W. Bush presidency and now the Barack Obama presidency.

It appears that when it comes to commutable distance, that was a strong term and strong standard within the George W. Bush presidency. Yet it appears that, currently, under the current administration, that component isn't necessarily so. What caused that? How is that interpretation so different?

Mr. WASHBURN. Thank you, Congressman Cárdenas. You know, the commutable distance standard is inherently arbitrary, too, because what is commutable to someone in California is not necessarily to someone in Oklahoma, for example. And so, frankly, it was a ambiguous and unclear standard.

It also presumes that the reason we have Indian gaming is to create jobs for Indian people. And that is part of the reason we have Indian gaming. But, frankly, again, as Ranking Member Hanabusa indicated, you know, $28 billion is another good reason to have Indian gaming. And that, you know, has nothing to do with the jobs at the casino. So, tribes tend to benefit from Indian gaming, even if it is not a commutable distance.

That doesn't mean we should be putting casinos up long distance from reservations. But the commutable distance just isn't necessarily a defensible standard.

Mr. CÁRDENAS. OK. Now, but when it comes to Indian gaming, I think that, to me, the term that I would use, it is about self-reliance. And without that kind of ability, most of the tribal lands in this country, where the reservations have been relegated to the most desolate, usually desert, usually mountainous, not necessarily prone to being able to grow saleable products, et cetera, et cetera, it is about self-reliance.

And, unfortunately, people in Indian Country, reservations, today are having to try to figure out how they create self-reliance. You know, selling beads on a reservation, as far as I know, has never really been something that an entire community could rely on for self-reliance and sustainability. So, to me, gaming, whether people like it or not, unfortunately for too many tribes around this country, that has been something that today seems to be the most viable opportunity for one community to be able to sustain itself.

But one of the things that I would like to ask you, have we had yet a situation where a tribe had petitioned to acquire lands, ended up using it for gaming, and it had a detrimental effect on another tribe's gaming facility?

Mr. WASHBURN. Well, it is possible that has happened. You know, we do all of our work up front, and then we make a decision. And then we don't end up having reasons to study it afterwards to determine what was the outcome. You know, did we guess right about detrimental impact?

Any time a new business opens up near another business, it may have, you know, a detrimental impact on the first business. You know, Wal-Mart is thinking about coming into Washington, DC, and I think the Target stores are probably kind of upset about that. And so, you know, that is inevitable. That doesn't necessarily mean we should block Wal-Marts from coming into Washington, DC, at least for that reason.

So, you know, I am sure that there are cases. I would guess that there may very well be cases where there has been a negative impact on existing businesses. But you know, as you said, some tribes are very poor, and this is the only opportunity they have. And just because another tribe is already up and running, doesn't necessarily mean we should keep the new tribe, the second tribe, from opening a casino in that area.

Mr. CÁRDENAS. Well, unfortunately, I think that the correct way to put it is most tribes in this country are very poor, not some. The vast, vast majority. And it is unfortunate that most Americans think that all Native American Nations in this country now each have a casino and they are all very well developed and there is sustained, self-reliance for that particular nation.

So, my time is up, and hopefully we have another opportunity to delve into this issue. Thank you very much, Mr. Chairman. I yield back.

Mr. YOUNG. Thank you. Mr. DeFazio.

Mr. DEFAZIO. Thank you, Mr. Chairman. I guess my question is, and I came in late, I apologize if you have already covered this. But when you have the not detrimental to the surrounding community, and now we just had a discussion and response to my colleague's question about negative impact on an existing business, and you are saying in some cases that is not detrimental, so I am trying to understand what the not detrimental to the surrounding community means, in terms of impact on existing businesses, particularly if it was another tribe who had an established gaming facility nearby.

Mr. WASHBURN. Thank you, Ranking Member DeFazio. You know, detrimental is sort of a balancing act. On balance, does the casino, or the proposed gaming operation on balance, you know, have a overall cumulative negative effect or a cumulative positive effect. And for many communities, they are very much in favor of the development, because it is going to bring jobs to the community, it is going to bring construction to the community, it is going to bring development to the community.

So, there will, in almost every community, there is a group of people that are opposed, and there is a group of people in favor. And so we have to kind of balance that out and figure out what's the net. Is it net detrimental, or is it net positive? And it is not a scientific analysis, it is the analysis that Congress gave us when it used that language, "detrimental impact." I blame Chairman Young for that.

[Laughter.]

Mr. DeFazio. Really?

[Laughter.]

Mr. DeFazio. Don? Do you have a—no, never—you were just blamed for the vague determination of what is detrimental to a surrounding community.

Mr. Young. Frank Ducheneaux did that. I will blame him.

[Laughter.]

Mr. DeFazio. OK. Reclaiming my time, then, so there is no, like, specific regulatory guidance? I mean do you have precedence you go back and look at? I mean, I am just trying to get—I mean, because it—you know, this is your political—and as the job—you know, people—you go from administration to administration, I am just wondering. How much can this swing?

Mr. Washburn. Well, we certainly are prohibited by law from behaving in an arbitrary and capricious fashion. So we have to——

Mr. DeFazio. But does that mean you have to be consistent?

Mr. Washburn. Well, at least somewhat consistent, because——

Mr. DeFazio. Oh, somewhat. OK.

Mr. Washburn [continuing]. Too inconsistent would be arbitrary. And, by the way, as to that analysis, the Governor, of course, gets to make the final call, the Governor of the State. So the Governor ultimately can say whether it is detrimental or not, too, if the Governor chooses.

So, if the Governor disagrees, the Governor can give the thumbs down, even though we have approved one of those two-part determinations. So I am not the only political actor involved in those decisions.

Mr. DeFazio. And if a Governor does that, what is the recourse at that point?

Mr. Washburn. It is done. It is done. They don't——

Mr. DeFazio. That is not litigable?

Mr. Washburn. I don't believe, I don't think that the Governors' actions have been litigated. I don't recall a case where that has been the case, because it is pretty much purely a political decision of the Governor. And so, I haven't seen that, and I pay attention to this field a fair bit.

Mr. DeFazio. Right. Are there any, and, again, I apologize for not being here earlier and thoroughly read all the materials you provided. But, I mean, are there major pending cases that might lead to further reinterpretation of the two-part process?

Mr. WASHBURN. Well, I wouldn't say that we are looking to do any reinterpretation of the process. The process has been, you know, has been working since 1988. It doesn't work often. I mean it doesn't happen often. But it, you know, it is imperfect, it has some ambiguous terms, and we have tried to define those in our regulations. But——

Mr. DEFAZIO. But you did have changes in—when you had the commuting standard, that was sort of overruled or discarded after some controversy, et cetera.

Mr. WASHBURN. Yes. We don't foresee making any major policy guidance in that area. We have tried to look at our past decisions and be consistent with what we have done in the past. And, you know, I have had the opportunity to make one of these decisions fairly recently. And we consider these things fairly carefully.

So the most recent decision we issued is about 53 pages long and it has got more than 360 footnotes citing how we considered all the factors. And that is just the opinion letter. There is also a record of decision that is 50 pages plus several stacks of notebooks of supporting documents. So these are very difficult exercises. And they are very carefully considered.

I am not saying that we get it right every time, but we do consider them very carefully. And that is a process that has really grown since IGRA. We give more attention to these nowadays. And over time it seems like we produce a lot more paper and a lot more rigorous study than we did when we first started doing this.

Mr. DEFAZIO. OK. Thank you, Mr. Chairman.

Mr. YOUNG. I thank the gentleman. Kevin, recently, I believe it was August 23, you approved an off-reservation Class III casino in the city of Kenosha, Wisconsin, for a tribe more than 160 miles from an existing reservation headquarters. It is my understanding the secretarial determination found that the proposed gaming facility would be in the best interest of the tribe and its members, but not detrimental to the surrounding community.

It appears that your approval of this project minimizes, ignores the negative impacts of neighboring tribes, including the Potawatomi, the City and County of Milwaukee, and Northern Illinois. I have read reports where estimating an off-reservation casino would cause a loss of up to 3,000 jobs in Milwaukee, and reduce the revenues of other tribes.

How, again, did you personally or your agency, or was it done by an independent study, approve this off-reservation casino, when it definitely does have detrimental consequences?

Mr. WASHBURN. Well, Chairman, we considered carefully the views of everybody that weighed in on that decision. And, you know, again, that is the decision I was referring to, and I misspoke, it is actually 56 pages long, I think, with 360 footnotes. And we very carefully went through the information that was submitted to us by all parties.

It is a situation where everybody that was within the 25-mile limit, or not everybody, but many people within the 25-mile limit, were very, very much in favor of this casino and the economic development that it would spawn.

Mr. YOUNG. With all due respect, who was in favor? The County of Milwaukee is against it——

Mr. WASHBURN. Well——

Mr. YOUNG [continuing]. The city of Milwaukee was against it, the tribes were against it. Who was in favor of it?

Mr. WASHBURN. Well, it wasn't located in Milwaukee, and it wasn't located within the County of Milwaukee either. It was located within the city of Kenosha. And that county and that city were very much in favor of it.

And it was, you know, to be fair, I met with many people from Milwaukee, even though they were not within the 25-mile zone. I met the mayor from Milwaukee while considering this decision. I met many members of the city council and, frankly, many members of the State legislature. Several leaders in the State legislature came to see me. And I listened to all of them and thought through their arguments very carefully.

You know, ultimately, we haven't made a final decision on that, because we haven't actually made the decision to take the land into trust. But we have made the decision to ask Governor Walker whether he would care to approve this, because we have sent it to him for a decision because we do think that this would be in the interest of the Menominee tribe, and not detrimental to the surrounding community, as defined by our regulation.

Mr. YOUNG. Now, the Governor has to approve this? And a Class III has to be approved by the Governor?

Mr. WASHBURN. That is right. Well, that is right. The tribe has to have a Class III gaming compact, which I believe they already have, because they have got another operation. But yes, they have to have the Governor's approval for the two-part determination.

Mr. YOUNG. Again I go back to my interests here. When you build a casino, you borrow the money, you have approved it yourself, they go forth and invest. They take the money and spend. And this is all right for the tribe.

But now you have a tribe 160 miles away that has their own casino and jumps over to try to be in competition in one casino. Now, if that is the case, why don't you let the tribe that is in Milwaukee jump over and have a casino there? And when it is applied for?

Mr. WASHBURN. Well, Chairman, the tribe in Milwaukee, it was a very successful tribe. And the precedent of them was very compelling, frankly. The Forest County Potawatomi Tribe had a reservation that was more than 200 miles away from Milwaukee. And when they got one of the very first off-reservation——

Mr. YOUNG. Many years ago.

Mr. WASHBURN [continuing]. Gaming operations many years ago, and it has been roughly 20 years, and they have had a really successful run. And we determined, based on economic analysis provided to us, that it wouldn't have very much impact on them. And by the way, they were not within the 25-mile zone, they were further——

Mr. YOUNG. By the way, we are going to change the 25-mile zone. Because I know the original intent was never 25 miles, and I wrote this damn bill. And it was never meant, I know a little bit about this business, and you have to have a certain market. And my concern is if we keep doing this off-reservation gambling, you keep approving them, eventually the States are going to say, "The hell with it. We will legalize gambling." And there are only so many dollars out there to be lost to those slot machines. I lose most of them, by the way.

But the other thing, and I believe it is Oregon, we talked about that, I believe, the Cow Creek Tribe in Oregon is facing a difficult situation. I am concerned, if we are not careful, it will become an epidemic across the country. The tribe faces a threat from a neighboring tribe, which already operates a casino on its own aboriginal lands, and is attempting to jump over and open a second casino on non-aboriginal lands. The second casino would cut into Cow Tribe's market and lead to the loss of over 500 jobs.

Do you guys really look at this, or do you have someone who is your main man that does this? Not you.

Mr. WASHBURN. Well, we have an Office of Indian Gaming that does a lot, you know, that prepares this for us. But, ultimately, you know, yes, I mean, these decisions get a lot of attention from me. I spent, you know, a weekend, a couple of weekends, working on this one. I didn't write it all myself, but these are decisions that we take very seriously.

And, frankly, they are the kind of decisions that I am going to be called over to Congress to answer for. So I take them very seriously and give them a great deal of attention, even while I am dealing with social services, and schools, and police, and all the other things that we deal with.

Mr. YOUNG. Would it be helpful, again, I still think the committee is somewhat interested, would it be helpful to us to review this IGRA law and see, maybe put the distance in it, take this burden off your back and maybe rewrite the law so it works a little better?

Mr. WASHBURN. You know, writing the law is your responsibility and applying it is my responsibility.

Mr. YOUNG. I mean I am asking you. Do you like what it is now?

Mr. WASHBURN. We believe it is workable the way it is now. With all the——

Mr. YOUNG. It is workable? Or is it easy to be worked?

Mr. WASHBURN. That is a good question. We are not asking you to amend IGRA, but we certainly respect your power to do so. And we can work, we have been working with it since 1988. So 25 years. And we have managed to make our peace with it and we can apply it.

But I think these are inherently controversial decisions. And so, whatever the mileage figure would be, it would be controversial. And if you take it up, they will be yelling at you a little bit, as well.

Mr. YOUNG. We are paid the same amount, but probably you are paid more, but I would say that maybe, let's put it this way. Would your so-called legal group like to help us as we rewrite a piece of legislation to clarify this issue? Because I don't think we can continue the suspension of gambling casinos by Native tribes.

Because, and by the way, I have a case in California, in Colusa County. I think you are aware of it. Don't do that, because here comes the guy out of Illinois, financing the whole project, has a small tribe that is going to move into an existing casino area. And who is going to benefit from it? Not going to be the tribe. These are shyster investors.

And I am just saying, you know, there are only so many ounces of blood in every turnip. And we can't continue this or we will flood the market with gambling, and it will all go broke. And that is, the tribes, because this is a revenue base, it is working well. And I don't want us to keep putting the burden on the poor camel to the point it falls down. I mean it just won't carry it. And I am just saying let's step back a while. I hope you understand, let's step back a while. Let's review this.

Now you say the Governor, I don't always trust these Governors. Very frankly, they may make revenue for themselves or for the State. They shouldn't have the last say. Maybe we ought to make it the State legislature. Maybe you ought to be working with us on this.

Mr. LaMalfa, do you have another question?

Mr. LaMalfa. Yes, sir.

Mr. Young. Go ahead.

Mr. LaMalfa. Thank you, Mr. Chairman. Following back up with the process here, the company AES, in the various off-reservation projects that they have vetted and covered over the years, our information has it they have never found any off-reservation, one project that they deemed having any kind of detrimental effect on other neighboring tribes, whether you are talking 25 miles or whatever the number is. Our understanding is every report ever made is they have not found detrimental effects.

And so, I wondered what your experience is with that. Do you agree that they have never found any, and instead of recommending going forward that there wouldn't be any effects, either, say environmentally, or certainly on surrounding tribes?

Mr. Washburn. Congressman, I have, you know, I have been in this position only about a year. So I haven't seen the vast run of their work, of this particular economist's work. So I am not capable of answering that question. But you know, we figure that everybody has a self-interested reason for providing us information. And that is the way the world works. And so, you know, we bring a healthy skepticism to everything we read in this area, and evaluate it as best we can. So, you know, that is kind of the way it is.

You know, a lot of people think the government shouldn't be in the business of making economic decisions, but we do the best we can with the staff that we have. And, you know, I feel like, for the most part, we do a good job. Again, we don't go back after the fact and do investigations to figure out whether we were right or wrong.

Mr. LaMalfa. I am not saying that a bad job is being done. I just think maybe the criteria, the base line, needs to be relooked at, and that in a case where a group is being contracted to do the study that you are using as perhaps a big portion of your information, but also is going to be the same group that has the interest in building the project, you know, because, again, we have information that shows that these are the same folks that are contracted to build a project that then are producing an EIS or the impact study that has a major component of what you are using to base decisions on, whether it is impact or not.

So, again, it really cries out for revamping, whether it is that geographic zone of mileage, or a separation, you know, something that has more third-party in the process, because in other areas I certainly, with environmental things that, I wish farmers and ranchers could produce their own studies and have the environmental groups, or regulatory agencies use those——

Mr. YOUNG. Will the gentleman yield?

Mr. LAMALFA. Yes, sir.

Mr. YOUNG. The one company, and I believe, Wisconsin, you used an 8-year-old EIS study when you issued that permit. I don't know if you are aware of that. Eight years old. That is kind of outdated. And yet you issued it and took the land in trust.

Mr. WASHBURN. Well, Chairman, that is evidence of how long these decisions take to get out. We consider them for many, many years. But whenever, we always ask, we always ended up having to—those do go stale. And they have to be redone after a certain period of time. And we determined that one, there was some additional work that had to be done to make sure that one was not stale.

Mr. YOUNG. I thank the gentleman. Go ahead, I am sorry. But 8 years seems like a long time.

Mr. LAMALFA. It certainly does. But again, coming back to that, we have the same people producing documents you might be using in the decision, they are also the ones that are contracting for it. Does that really, I mean would that really pass the smell test in a lot of other examples of regulatory environment and government?

Mr. WASHBURN. Well, the question, really, is should the taxpayers bear the cost of the environmental review, or should the people that are proposing the project? And we believe that cost should be borne by the people who are, you know, pushing the project forward, rather than being borne by the taxpayers. And so——

Mr. LAMALFA. Certainly, but independently or using their hand-picked ones?

Mr. WASHBURN. Well, we give an independent review of those things. And we have different processes that we use, depending on the context. But we sometimes are involved in choosing. We require them to provide us choices in certain circumstances——

Mr. LAMALFA. OK. Back on my own time here, but when you have a group that has never found a detrimental effect for a project it is interested in on other neighboring tribes or environmental, then that would be a red flag that I would wish you would, you know, consider more often in the process. So thank you.

Mr. WASHBURN. Thank you, Congressman.

Mr. YOUNG. We have a vote on, but we have some time. Madam Chair, you would like—go ahead.

Dr. RUIZ. Thank you very much. Dr. Washburn, you mentioned that you do a very thorough environmental economic impact to the surrounding communities. My question is, do you also assess the economic impact of the other tribes in the area? And that is the first part.

Second is what is the mechanism for their input into this process?

Mr. WASHBURN. Thank you, Congressman. Well, we consider the views of other tribes if they make them known to us. And, again, if they are within the 25-mile zone for a two-part determination, we automatically consider their input. If they aren't within the 25-

mile area, then they have to petition for their views to be considered. And sometimes tribes do petition, and sometimes they don't.

I will tell you that as Assistant Secretary for Indian Affairs, I don't turn down tribal leaders who come to my office and ask for a meeting, you know, really, about anything. I think it is my duty and my job, and I enjoy it, meeting with tribal leaders. And so, you know, they tend to make their views known to me, and they don't get ignored, they get heard.

And you know, we don't make very many of these decisions. This is, you know, one of the very rare things that we do.

Dr. RUIZ. You know, as a physician, that has worked to relieve disparities and improve health care access for a lot of medically under-served communities, I work a lot with Federal qualified health centers. And in order for a new Federal qualified health center to enter a community, they need to get letters of support from the surrounding FQHC's to bring it in as a community and agreement. And this really allows them the opportunity to have conversations within the other FQHC's to talk about what kind of services they can collaborate on, et cetera, to make sure that we create, we maximize the value for everybody. Would that be a possibility?

Mr. WASHBURN. Thank you, Congressman. That is a beautiful model. And it would be a vast improvement if tribes sort of worked more cooperatively with one another about these matters, for sure. And we love it when we see that happening.

We don't always see it happening. And even when we don't see it happening, we still have to make decisions. And so, we make positive decisions sometimes when there are people who oppose. And we wish that we always had consensus. And we look for consensus. Consensus is a very good thing in this area. In fact, when we make these decisions and there is broad consensus, nobody even hardly notices, it seems like. It is the ones that have a lot of conflict around them, those are the ones that get a lot of attention.

So, we would love to see more tribes working together on these kinds of gaming operations.

Dr. RUIZ. Thank you very much. I yield my time.

Mr. YOUNG. Madam.

Ms. HANABUSA. Thank you, Mr. Chair. Mr. Washburn, I just have a couple of small follow-up questions. One was, you want to come back?

Mr. YOUNG. We have to, because there is another panel.

Ms. HANABUSA. Oh, I know that.

When a tribe goes off-reservation, do they have to have some kind of relationship with the lands to which they are going? Like they have cultural ties or some kind of a tie?

Mr. WASHBURN. Yes, Congressman, Ranking Member. That is an important factor that we consider any time that a tribe wishes to go off the reservation.

Ms. HANABUSA. So are you looking for some kind of historical connection? What do you call it——

Mr. WASHBURN. Well, a historical or cultural connection to the land. And it is an important factor. It is not the sole factor, but it is a very important factor that we consider.

Ms. HANABUSA. And when you do, any kind of a request that comes to you to go off-reservation also has to comply with NEPA. I think you said that earlier, right?

Mr. WASHBURN. That is—yes, ma'am.

Ms. HANABUSA. Who is the final accepting agency, or the person who makes a determination that the environmental impact statement is sufficient and in compliance?

Mr. WASHBURN. That would be us. We have to review that NEPA analysis very carefully. And if we don't think it is an adequate analysis, we send it back. And we ultimately have to be satisfied with that analysis. And that is sort of an iterative process. We take a look at it and say, "We don't think you have done a good enough job in this section or that section. We need more information." And so that tends to happen. We don't take it just as written the first time it comes in.

Ms. HANABUSA. Have you ever been challenged on the acceptance of an EIS as sufficient, and someone say that you hadn't considered or it was inadequate, and therefore it doesn't then meet the criteria of what needs to happen before you can go and make a determination of the two-part test?

Mr. WASHBURN. I believe we have, Madam Ranking Member. I think that is a common subject in litigation. So it does come up, and we have Federal courts looking over our shoulders. Another reason we really feel it better be adequate, and we better make sure it is adequate. Otherwise, we are vulnerable to having our decision overturned.

Ms. HANABUSA. So, is one of the criteria that you look for when you evaluate the sufficiency of the environmental impact statement whether impact, the economic impact, has been considered, as well as the social impact and cultural impacts, or all the normal criteria? Are you looking for all of those points to be addressed in the environmental impact statement?

Mr. WASHBURN. Yes, Madam Ranking Member. There are a number of things that we have to consider. And I think it is fair to say that, at least in general, those are the kinds of things that do have to be considered. There is a fair bit of detail, and it is a very elaborate, complex process. But those are the kinds of considerations that we have to look into.

Ms. HANABUSA. Thank you. Mr. Chair, I yield.

Mr. YOUNG. If the gentlelady will listen to this question, now, Kevin, she asked a question about aboriginal connection. The one in Oregon, there was no aboriginal connection with the tribe that went there. That is a fact. That was not aboriginal land. I mean because if there is an aboriginal connection, that is important. But when they take land into trust that had no aboriginal lineage to the one tribe that applied for it, you failed. You can talk to your lawyers, that was not their land. They never had any relation to it at all.

Mr. WASHBURN. Well, Chairman, it is one of the very serious factors we consider. And I don't know the specific details of the matter that you are referring to, and I suspect it may be in litigation. But it is a factor that we take very seriously. And it is not the only factor, so there may be extremely compelling other factors that could outweigh that factor. But it is one of the factors that we consider very carefully.

Mr. YOUNG. I would suggest respectfully, Kevin, and you know I have talked to you before about this, I would back off until we look at what has happened. Because this outfit that is doing your work, I don't know anything about them. It wasn't just you. This has been going on for a period of time. And I would suggest respectfully that there may be a little something going on that shouldn't be going on.

I am a person that wants to have a casino, and I am from Illinois. I like it because Chicago is involved, so I go find a tribal member over here, and I have him apply over here in a good market. And the same bunch that does the study, has been doing all these studies, and the gentleman from California, no one has ever said there would be a detrimental effect. That is sort of interesting, to have someone say that. No detriment, none, no case that we know of, that the same company, so the next time we may have this company here, because you guys aren't really doing this. You hired somebody to do it. You review it. And most of the time you accept it.

So, I am just suggesting, respectfully, as the Assistant Secretary, you should be full Secretary, not because you should be a Secretary of the Interior. My job is you should be a cabinet member. Not you, particularly, but the position. I mean——

Mr. WASHBURN. Well, wait a minute, Mr. Chairman——

Mr. YOUNG [continuing]. This would be good. Yes. But you follow what I am saying? I don't want this abundance of gambling casinos to occur in competition with other tribes. Competition is good. You said you set the market. Well, OK. But you have a trust, too. So if they fail, guess who is going to pick the tab up? We are.

By the way, it has not been funded adequately; I hope you tell the President of that. I mean the Park Service had an increase of 28 percent and Fish and Wildlife 29 percent. You had a little tiny bit in the Department of the Interior. Not good. I want to take that money from them and give it to you and see how much of a martyr you will be when you get offered how many more billion dollars. Let's see how good you can operate this show.

Anyway, does anybody have any other questions?

[No response.]

Mr. YOUNG. I want to thank you, Kevin. And communicate with us. Because I do think possibly there will be legislation down the line to try to rectify it. I think it is an over-abundance of those outside that are being financed by people I question to have too many gambling casinos by Indian tribes. Maybe we will set up a deal where everybody can share in the wealth. They do this in California. They do it in Arizona. But other places they don't do it. So that is something. I want to thank you.

And the rest of the panel, please wait. We will be back here in about, I would say, right about 4:00. So maybe a little sooner. So be around. Thank you.

Mr. WASHBURN. Thank you, Chairman.

[Recess.]

Mr. YOUNG. The committee will come to order. Again, I apologize to the witnesses. This is the problem of this Congress we serve in. There is little awareness of how we are going to run it.

So anyway, at this time I would like to welcome Honorable Todd Mielke; Ms. Hazel Longmire; and Mr. Alexander Skibine. OK, and we will start with you, Todd. You are the first one up. I think you know the rules, but I am pretty lenient. If you are really doing something intelligent, I will give you some more time.

[Laughter.]

Mr. MIELKE. Thank you.

Mr. YOUNG. So if I bang the gavel, don't feel offended. Go ahead, sir.

Mr. MIELKE. I will try to live up to that expectation. Thank you.

STATEMENT OF TODD MIELKE, COUNTY COMMISSIONER, COUNTY OF SPOKANE

Mr. MIELKE. Good afternoon, Mr. Chairman and members of the committee. For the record, my name is Todd Mielke. I am a Spokane County Commissioner, and currently serve as the President of the Washington State Association of Counties. Today I am speaking on behalf of Spokane County, the city of Spokane, and Greater Spokane, Incorporated, our region's largest Chamber of Commerce. I want to discuss our experience with the Bureau of Indian Affairs and off-reservation gaming.

Spokane County generally enjoys a constructive working relationship with other governmental jurisdictions, including local tribal governments. But that doesn't mean we always agree. On the question of whether one of our local tribes should be allowed to open an off-reservation casino, however, the county is deeply frustrated.

It is our view that BIA's policy toward off-reservation gaming has changed dramatically in a relatively short period of time. It appears to have abandoned the principle that off-reservation gaming is to be the rare exception. Section 20 was included in IGRA to prevent the unfettered expansion of off-reservation casinos.

The interpretation of IGRA has historically been to start from the perspective that off-reservation gaming is prohibited. In fact, the Department not only supported limiting the expansion of gaming, it presented a plan to Congress to restrict gaming to reservations. And the exceptions to the gaming prohibition were to be narrowly interpreted to permit landless and newly recognized tribes to have the opportunity to have casinos in their historic territories, not to permit tribes to expand beyond tribal lands, because other locations were potentially more lucrative. And local jurisdictions were given deference in helping determine what was best for their community.

Today, due to our own experience, it appears that those prior standards are in question. The Department is no longer an objective arbitrator of whether any standards are being met. The Department is clearly seen as a project proponent.

One of the two primary standards applied to any permit for off-reservation gaming is whether there is detriment to the surrounding community. We have spent hundreds of thousands of dollars in data analysis, only to have the Department apparently dismiss it. Jurisdictions representing 99 percent of Spokane County's residents opposed this project, due to detriments they perceive. The regional offices disregard of the impacts on the surrounding community is not permitted under IGRA, in our view.

The overwhelming regional opposition should have resulted in a finding of detriment, and denial of the proposal. Yet the Department has stated that public sentiment is not a legitimate basis for denying an application.

This raises several significant questions. Who gets to define "detriment"? The local community in which the proposed off-reservation casino is to be located, or the BIA? And what happens when we believe that a proposed off-reservation casino would have deep, unmitigatable negative impacts and the BIA disagrees? Detriment has to mean something, and local government officials need to play a role in defining what that means for their jurisdiction.

If the new approach for BIA is that the default position is to approve all applications for off-reservation gaming, there will be consequences. This new approach will be a race where tribes attempt to leap-frog to better locations for market reasons, undermining the investments of other tribes, and the impacts on the community at large. Off-reservation gaming will no longer be the exception to the rule; it will be the rule.

I would like to provide some context. More than a decade ago, the Spokane Tribe filed a request with BIA to have 145 acres of land within our county acquired in trust. The county opposed the trust application because it did not want gaming on the proposed site. The tribe assured the county and the public that it did not plan to develop gaming on that site. So, without headquarters review or an EIS, the BIA acquired the land in trust. But in 2007, the tribe began to pursue a massive gaming operation on the site, which would include a 300-room hotel tower, a number of restaurants and bars, a convention area, and a significant retail complex.

What is at stake is tremendously important: Fairchild Air Force Base. Spokane County is home to the only Air Force tanker base in the Western Continental U.S. Congress and the Air Force have invested more than $200 million in capital improvements at the base in the past decade. Fairchild is the largest single-site employer in Spokane, with more than 5,000 employees, and has an economic impact of approximately $1.5 billion, annually.

The tribe, however, has proposed to build its casino resort 8/10 of a mile from the base's only runway, and less than 1,000 feet directly beneath the tanker flight training path. Basic common sense tells us that building a resort casino that expects to see thousands of visitors each day will undermine the base's ability to conduct effective real-life mission training. It is difficult to imagine an activity less consistent with the needs of a military base that trains tanker pilots in day and night operations with a brightly lit casino with thousands of visitors less than 1,000 feet below.

The Spokane Tribe is not a landless tribe, nor does it lack for revenue from its business enterprises. It has one of the largest reservations in the Northwest, with more than 165,000 acres of vast timber and natural resource holdings, in addition to other casinos and a reported $54 million in annual revenue, based on their tribal enterprises in 2011.

I want the Spokane Tribe to succeed. And in my experience, they are highly effective at advocating for their interests. But I can't, as a representative of over 485,000 residents in Spokane County, support something I know will be detrimental to their future.

In closing, Spokane County's view is that the process is broken. If the Department can conclude siting a casino less than 1,000 feet directly beneath military training operations, and which is opposed by 99 percent of the residents of the region, will not be detrimental to the surrounding community, the detriment standard has no meaning. Thank you very much for the opportunity to speak to you today.

[The prepared statement of Mr. Mielke follows:]

PREPARED STATEMENT OF TODD MIELKE, COUNTY COMMISSIONER, COUNTY OF SPOKANE

My name is Todd Mielke. I am a Spokane County Commissioner and currently serve as the President of the Washington State Association of Counties. Today I am speaking on behalf of Spokane County, Washington to discuss our experience with the Bureau of Indian Affairs and off-reservation gaming.

Spokane County enjoys generally constructive working relationships with other government jurisdictions, including local tribal governments, though that doesn't mean we always agree. On the question of whether the Spokane Tribe should be allowed to open an off-reservation casino, however, the County is deeply frustrated.

The County meets the criteria of the Department of the Interior's definition of an "appropriate local official" in the regulations it uses to implement section 20 of the Indian Gaming Regulatory Act (IGRA). As such, the County has provided written evidence of the clear and unambiguous detriment that the Spokane Tribe's proposed off-reservation casino would cause to Spokane County and the citizens we represent.

And while the BIA accommodated our and other local governments' efforts to submit evidence of the great harm that would be caused to our community as a result of the Spokane Tribe's proposal, we are very concerned that, at least up to this point, the BIA's process has not given those concerns the weight they deserve in determining whether or not to allow the Spokane Tribe to move forward. Why do I say this? Because the County has been informed that BIA's Regional Director has recommended that the Secretary issue a finding that the proposed casino will not be detrimental to the surrounding community despite the overwhelming evidence to the contrary.

This raises several very significant questions: who gets to define detriment? The local community in which the proposed off-reservation casino is to be located—or the BIA? And what happens when, as in our case, we believe that a proposed off-reservation casino would have deep, un-mitigatable negative impacts and the BIA disagrees? I would submit that detriment has to mean something and that local government officials need to play a role in defining what that means for their jurisdiction.

I'd like to provide some context. More than a decade ago, the Spokane Tribe filed a request with the Bureau of Indian Affairs to have 145 acres of Spokane County land acquired in trust. The County opposed the trust acquisition because it did not want gaming on the proposed site. The tribe, however, assured the County and the public that it did not plan to develop a casino. So without headquarters review or an EIS, the BIA acquired the land in trust. By 2007, however, the tribe began to pursue a massive gaming operation on the site which would also include a 300-room hotel tower, a number of restaurants and bars, a convention/banquet area, and a significant retail complex.

The Spokane Tribe is not a landless tribe, nor does it lack for revenue from its business enterprises. In fact, it has one of the largest reservations in the Northwest, with more than 165,000 acres, including vast timber and other natural resource holdings. In addition, the tribe has two other casinos and reported $54 million in revenue for their Tribal Enterprises in 2011. I want the Spokane Tribe to succeed, and in my experience, they are highly effective at advocating for their interests. But I can't, as a representative of the over 485,000 residents of Spokane County support something that I know will be so detrimental to their future.

The opposition to the Tribe's proposal is extraordinary. In addition to the County, jurisdictions representing the vast majority of the area's residents including the nearby Cities of Spokane and Cheney have written to oppose the Spokane Tribe's proposed off-reservation casino because of the great harm it would cause their governments and their citizens. Additionally, the BIA has received letters opposing the tribe's development from U.S. Representative Cathy McMorris Rogers; the current and former Secretaries of the State of Washington; numerous State Senators and Representatives, and the Spokane Chamber of Commerce, known as Greater Spokane Inc. Yet the Department has stated that public sentiment is not a legitimate basis for denying an application.

Only the city of Airway Heights, which represents less than 5,000—or 1 percent—of the region's residents, supports the project. And only Airway Heights will receive any mitigation for the impacts the project would generate.

What's at stake is tremendously important—Fairchild Air Force Base. Spokane County is home to the only Air Force tanker base in the Western Continental United States. The base is responsible for refueling missions throughout the world, but is particularly important strategically for protecting the Nation's western borders. It is also the economic driver of the region. Fairchild is the largest single site employer in Spokane and has an economic impact of approximately $1.5 billion annually.

The tribe, however, has proposed to build its casino and hotel tower $9/10$ of a mile from the Base's only runway, and less than a 1,000 feet directly beneath the tanker flight training path. Basic common sense dictates that building a casino and hotel tower that expect to see thousands of visitors each day will undermine the Base's ability to conduct effective, real-life mission training. Indeed, it is difficult to imagine an activity less consistent with the needs of a military base that trains tanker pilots in day and night operations than siting a brightly lit casino with thousands of visitors less than a 1,000 feet beneath training approaches. The County's land use regulations do not permit any concentrated development like what the tribe is contemplating at the proposed site. Nor do the recently adopted Joint Land Use Study regulations adopted by all the regional jurisdictions in collaboration with the Department of Defense, except the city of Airway Heights, which has deviated from all other jurisdictions and within whose boundaries the casino-resort is proposed to be located.

The overwhelming regional opposition due to detriment should have resulted in a finding of detriment and a denial of the proposed gaming facility. Yet, as noted earlier, the Regional Director appears to have ignored this evidence and approved the project.

The Regional Office's disregard of the impacts on the surrounding community is not permitted under IGRA. Section 20 was included in IGRA to prevent the unfettered expansion of off-reservation casinos. The interpretation of IGRA has historically been to start from the perspective that off-reservation gaming is prohibited. In fact, the Department not only supported limiting the expansion of gaming, it presented a plan to Congress to restrict gaming to reservations. And the exceptions to the gaming prohibition were to be narrowly interpreted to permit landless and newly recognized tribes to have the opportunity to have casinos in their historic territories—not to permit tribes to expand beyond tribal lands because other locations were potentially more lucrative. And local jurisdictions were given deference in helping to determine what was best for their community.

Today, due to our own experience, it appears that those prior standards are in question. We have spent hundreds of thousands of dollars in data analysis only to have the Department apparently dismiss it, though, the BIA has informed the County that it is not permitted to see the Regional Director's decision.

In addition to how it determines community impacts, the Department changed how it evaluates the impact on tribes. Today, the department only measures whether the applicant tribe will be benefited and the calculation it conducts is simple—does the proposed site give the tribe greater access to a metropolitan area so that it can make more money? There is no longer consideration of whether another tribe has invested millions to develop a destination gaming resort on their reservation or whether is will be disadvantaged by being further away from metropolitan areas compared to their new competition. There is no longer consideration of whether a tribe that has previously met the standards for off-reservation gaming that the Department used to apply will be negatively impacted by this new competition. The end result of this new approach will be a race where tribes attempt to leap-frog to better locations, undermining the investments of other tribes and the impacts on the community at large. Off-reservation gaming will no longer be the exception to the rule—it will be the rule.

In a State where governmental services are funded through the collection of sales and property taxes generated in the community, the BIA's actions have the effect of diverting limited tax dollars to a non-taxpaying entity. The community is subsidizing the gaming operation whether it supports the activity or not. The result is fewer tax dollars available to pay for roads, criminal justice systems, local schools, public transportation, and social services.

In closing, Spokane County's view is that the process is broken. BIA's policy toward off-reservation gaming has changed dramatically in a relatively short period of time. It appears to have abandoned the principle that off-reservation gaming is to be the rare exception. The Department is no longer an objective arbitrator of whether any standards are being met. The Department is clearly a project proponent.

If the Department can conclude that a proposed off-reservation casino that would be located directly beneath military training operations and which is opposed by 99 percent of the region will not be detrimental to the surrounding community, the detriment standard is now meaningless.

Mr. YOUNG. I want to thank you, Todd. This is why we are having this hearing. There is no support for this. And I hope Mr. Washburn understands that. And if it appears that he does not, I guess we will have to step forward. Because nobody, including Cathy McMorris, supports this program. And I don't know where the Governor is. In fact, I don't even know who your Governor is right now. But Spokane is against it, the Air Force should be adamantly against it. I would not like to have that hotel built that close and be in one of those penthouse rooms. I wouldn't be in the penthouse, but somebody was there.

And so, thank you for your testimony. I appreciate it.

Mr. MIELKE. Thank you.

Mr. YOUNG. Ms. Hazel.

STATEMENT OF HAZEL LONGMIRE, VICE-CHAIRPERSON, COLUSA INDIAN COMMUNITY COUNCIL

Ms. LONGMIRE. Can you hear me now? Good afternoon, Mr. Chairman and members of the committee. I am the Vice-Chairperson of Colusa Indian Community Council in Colusa, California. Our tribe deeply appreciates this opportunity to share with you our experience with the way that the Department of the Interior and its Bureau of Indian Affairs has made so-called two-part determinations to take newly acquired lands into trust for gaming.

I am submitting a separate written statement documenting how, from our tribe's perspective, the Department of the Interior has acted as an untrustworthy trustee, by closing its eyes to the devastating impacts of its recent policies and decisions on tribes that have played by the rules and gone deeply into debt in the process.

Specifically, the Department now favors allowing tribes that already have gaming-eligible trust lands to move to better locations because their wealthy would-be casino developers prefer to finance only the most profitable projects.

First, our tribe believes that the Department of the Interior should accept land into Federal trust for tribes whose land trusts were taken, not voluntary sold or lost through termination. Or, if a tribe needs more land for housing, cultural purposes, or even economic development. In most cases, that sort of trust land acquisition is unlikely to have any significant impact on other tribes, unless the newly acquired land is within another tribe's traditional territory.

However, when it comes to acquiring new trust lands for gaming, IGRA clearly requires that the Department and BIA make an independent assessment of whether and how allowing each tribe to leapfrog over another tribe or tribes just to get a market advantage will impact those tribes being leapfrogged. The only way that the Department and BIA can make an independent assessment would be to consult directly with the existing tribes, rather than relying solely on an arbitrary definition of what constitutes nearby tribes.

The current process simply looks to the reports prepared by consultants, bought and paid for by project developers. When Enterprise Rancheria began its quest to put land into trust in Yuba County to build a casino, the Interior considered any tribe within a 50-mile radius to be nearby, and thus required consultation. However, in 2008 the Department shrank the radius within which tribes could be considered nearby to only 25 miles.

Our tribe is about 30 miles from the site of the proposed New Enterprise casino, and that casino would be in the heart of our primary market area, with far-better highway access. If Interior had only looked a few miles beyond their arbitrary 25-mile radius, they would have learned that Yuba County casino would likely reduce our casino's revenues by as much as 77 percent, and our tribal government's discretionary revenues by as much as 90 percent.

We repeatedly tried to bring these facts to the Department's attention, but we were either ignored or rebuffed. As recently as December 13, 2012, we wrote to Assistant Secretary Washburn to ask that he reconsider the decision or, in the alternative, defer accepting land into trust, pending the outcome of the lawsuit we proceeded to file. Ignoring the complexities of trying to unwind the Enterprise transaction if the court were to rule in our favor, the Department proceeded to full speed ahead.

Assistant Washburn has been quoted as saying that it is not his job to say no to Indian tribes. But when saying yes to one tribe is likely to devastate another tribe, we think that the Assistant Secretary has an obligation to take that impact into careful consideration, based on the Department's and the BIA's independent inquiry, rather than unquestionably rubber-stamping the result-driven conclusion of consultants, paid-for project proponents.

We don't think that IGRA needs to be changed. We do think that the way it is being implemented needs to be changed. Otherwise, all that we and other tribes in our area have worked so hard and long to accomplish will be lost so that a Chicago casino developer can reap millions of dollars in profits from selling land that it already owns at a price far above market value, and developing a casino that will seriously cannibalize the markets of other tribes that could not have seen it coming. Thank you.

[The prepared statement of Ms. Longmire follows:]

PREPARED STATEMENT OF HAZEL LONGMIRE, VICE CHAIRPERSON, COLUSA INDIAN
COMMUNITY COUNCIL, CACHIL DEHE BAND OF WINTUN INDIANS

My name is Hazel Longmire, and I am the Vice Chairperson the Cachil Dehe
Band of Wintun Indians of the Colusa Indian Community ("Colusa"). We are located
in rural Colusa County, California. Our tribe deeply appreciates this opportunity to
share with you our experience with the way that the Department of the Interior
("DOI") and its Bureau of Indian Affairs (BIA) has made so-called two-part determinations to take newly acquired land into trust for gaming purposes.

Unfortunately, I speak about the process from firsthand experience. On December
3, 2012, Assistant Secretary of the Interior—Indian Affairs Washburn published a
Federal Register notice that he had approved acquisition of off-reservation lands
for gaming purposes for the benefit of the Enterprise Rancheria and the North Fork
Rancheria in the Sacramento Valley and the San Joaquin Valley, respectively. We
write today to oppose the way that DOI and BIA currently are implementing "two-
part determinations" for off-reservation gaming acquisitions under 25 U.S.C. sec.
2719. We specifically oppose acquisition of off-reservation gaming lands for the Enterprise Rancheria because it threatens to destroy 30 years of hard work by our
tribe to lift itself from poverty just as we are succeeding in diversifying our tribal
economy.

Congress required consultation in two-part determinations under IGRA so that
DOI could not avoid consideration of the adverse impacts of off-reservation gaming
on nearby governments, including other Indian tribes. Section 20 of IGRA, 25 U.S.C.
§ 2719(b)(1)(A), requires that the Department consult not only with the Indian tribe
applying to permit gaming on off-reservation land acquired after October 17, 1988,
but also with "appropriate State and local officials, including officials of other nearby Indian tribes," to evaluate the detriment to the surrounding community of the
proposed casino. 25 U.S.C. § 2719(b)(1)(A). In its 2011 Record of Decision ("2011
ROD") approving Enterprise's application for a two-part determination, then-Assist-
ant Secretary Echo Hawk wrote that "[t]he Department also will apply heavy scrutiny to tribal applications for off-reservation gaming on lands acquired after October
17, 1988 to ensure that they do not result in a detrimental impact to communities
surrounding the proposed gaming site." 2011 ROD at 61 *(Please note that all Documents referenced herein are available at the Web site, https://sites.google.com/site/
longmiretestimony/).* He also made the categorical statement that "[t]he Department
will not approve a tribal application for off-reservation where a nearby Indian tribe
demonstrates that it is likely to suffer a detrimental impact as a result." *Id.* at 64.

Obviously, IGRA requires that DOI make an independent assessment of whether
and how allowing the applicant tribe will impact not just existing tribes' casinos,
but also the tribal governments and tribal citizens that depend on revenue from
those casinos. The only way that the DOI and BIA could make an independent assessment would be to consult directly with the tribes that may be affected, rather
than using an arbitrary definition of what constitutes "nearby" tribes without regard to actual conditions, and the result-driven reports prepared by consultants
bought and paid for by gaming developers. In BIA's own words, "[w]ithout early consultation, the Bureau may develop proposals based on an incomplete and anecdotal
understanding of the issues that surround a particular matter. As a result, Bureau
proposals often create severe unintended consequences for tribal governments." BIA
Government-to-Government Consultation Policy at 3 (2000)?. BIA's failure to consult
with our tribe led to just such unintended consequences when it approved Enterprise Rancheria's application to conduct off-reservation gaming on a site located not
only in the heart of our casino's primary market area, but between our Reservation
and our other major sources of patrons.

Yuba County Entertainment, LLC ("YCE"), the sole member of which is Forsythe
Racing, Inc., an Illinois corp. wholly owned by Gerald Forsythe of Chicago, Illinois,
owns extensive properties just south of Marysville, California, in unincorporated
Yuba County. The land YCE owns was approved by the voters of Yuba County as
a racetrack complex in 1998. Yuba County Board of Supervisors' Letter to BIA
(2009). In 2001, however, YCE began planning to use a portion of the racetrack land
for a casino with Enterprise as the beneficiary of the land, if not the recipient of
the lion's share of the profits. 2002 Enterprise Application at 164 (2001 Innovation
Group Report). After a decade of supposed analysis, DOI approved virtually the
same casino as proposed by YCE in 2002. Final Environmental Impact Statement,
Enterprise Rancheria Gaming Facility and Hotel Fee-To-Trust Acquisition (2009)
("EIS"), available at *http://enterpriseeis.com/documents/final_eis/report.htm.*

The Colusa Reservation is only 30 miles from the YCE parcel—closer to it than
Enterprise's own headquarters or reservation. During most of the time that the Enterprise application was pending with DOI, the definition of "nearby Indian tribes"

with which the Department was required to consult included all tribes within 50 miles. Checklist for Gaming Acquisitions at 7 (2007); 73 Fed. Reg. 29354, 29357 (2008) (discussing the 50-mile threshold in effect from 1997 through 2008). In 2008, DOI shrank the threshold for consultation with "appropriate State and local officials" and "nearby Indian tribes" from 50 to 25 miles. The new rule explained the decision to use 25 miles rather than 10 or 50 as the threshold for consulting with non-tribal governments. *Id.* DOI gave no notice or explanation for reducing the area within which it would consider Indian tribes to be "nearby" a proposed casino by a factor of 75 percent, however. Compare the final 25 CFR part 292 rule, 73 Fed. Reg. at 29357, adopting the 25-mile threshold, with the proposed rule including a 50-mile threshold, 65 Fed. Reg. 55471, 55473 (2000).

For the purpose of determining whether a tribe is in close proximity to a gaming establishment, DOI exercises a double standard. In evaluating "36 miles from the tribe's existing headquarters in Oroville, California" to the YCE parcel, DOI found that the distance was "relatively short," permitting the tribe to "regulate the conduct of class III gaming and exercise governmental power of the Site." Record of Decision; Secretarial Determination Pursuant to the Indian Gaming Regulatory Act for the 40-acre Yuba County site in Yuba County, California, for the Enterprise Rancheria (2011) ("2011 ROD") at 62; Record of Decision; Trust Acquisition of the 40-acre Yuba County site in Yuba County, California, for the Enterprise Rancheria of Maidu Indians of California (2012) ("2012 ROD"). Moreover, DOI found the YCE parcel to be "in relatively close proximity to the tribe's existing community," which is located almost entirely in Oroville. *Id.* at 41. Colusa, Mooretown, and Auburn's governments, lands, and people are actually closer to the proposed resort than either Enterprise's headquarters or its existing gaming-eligible reservation trust lands. *See e.g.,* Enterprise Lands in Context; Enterprise Lands in Context Google Maps *http://goo.gl/maps/LhUq7.*

After verbal requests for consultation were ineffective, Colusa formally requested consultation. Letter from Colusa Indian Community Council to BIA (2009). The BIA refused our request, hiding behind the new rule restricting "nearby Indian tribes" to those within 25 miles of the proposed off-reservation casino. Letter from BIA to Colusa Indian Community Council (2009). Instead of consulting with Colusa to determine whether it would be adversely affected, BIA invited Colusa to comment on the EIS along with other members of the public, essentially requiring Colusa to prove that it would be adversely affected before BIA would consult with it. *Id.* That violated both DOI's fiduciary responsibility to affected Indian tribes, and IGRA, which requires DOI to determine whether a proposed casino would adversely affect "nearby Indian tribes". In the 2008 rule, DOI wrote that "the purpose of consulting with nearby Indian tribes is to determine whether a proposed gaming establishment will have detrimental impacts on a nearby Indian tribe that is part of the surrounding community." 73 Fed. Reg. at 29356. The refusal by BIA to consult turned the purpose of consultation from a shield for tribes from adverse effects of Federal actions, to a shield for those Federal actions from candid discussion of those actions with the Departments' tribal trustees.

DOI had been on notice since at least Enterprise's 2002 application, however, that the proposed casino on YCE's land would "cannibalize" much of the business of other tribal casinos, including the Colusa Casino, and thus deprive the tribal governments that owned them of much-needed income to support services to their members. 2002 Enterprise Application at 164. Obviously, a Federal action that will lead to cannibalization of the business upon which a tribal government depends to support its membership is an adverse effect on its "governmental functions, infrastructure, and services." As demonstrated by the discussion of "cannibalization" in Appendix M to the FEIS, and indeed in Enterprise's original application, a 25-mile threshold is far too small to include all tribes affected by a new casino, because tribes whose business specifically would be targeted by YCE and Enterprise were generally farther than 25 miles away. EIS, Appendix M at 6 (2006) available at *http://enterpriseeis.com/documents/final_eis/files/appendices/vol1/ Appendix M.pdf* ("Appendix M"). Colusa submitted comments on the application and the EIS, but BIA never did consult with us. Moreover, the consultant responsible for preparing the Enterprise FEIS knew about the likely impacts on our casino, because we had used the same consultant in preparing a 2003 tribal EIS for a proposed expansion of our facility.

The total population of rural Colusa County is about 25,000. Because so few people live in Colusa County, most of our casino's customers come from Yuba City, Marysville and North Sacramento. Many of our employees also live in those same areas. In a rural area such as ours, people think nothing of driving 30 or 40 miles, but if Enterprise is allowed to leapfrog over us and open a casino on the YCE parcel near Marysville, our casino would sustain devastating reductions in revenues, with equally devastating impacts on our tribal government, our members and neighbors in Colusa County.

Enterprise's EIS guessed that the proposed Enterprise Casino in Yuba County would have a minor (between 3 percent and 7 percent) impact on what it supposed to be the gross revenues of Colusa's casino. It did not even try to guess at the impacts on the tribal government. The Enterprise EIS based that guess on purely hypothetical assumptions, without any actual data from the Colusa Casino concerning its revenues, costs of doing business or actual market area. At no time did the drafters of the EIS or BIA contact Colusa to determine what the actual effects on the tribe or its casino would be. As the drafters wrote: "much of the information contained in this report was received from third parties which Gaming Market Advisors did not validate or verify." Appendix M at 131.

Studies by nationally-renowned experts and based on empirical facts, however, have found that the proposed Enterprise Casino which will be located in the heart of the Colusa Casino's core market area, will have far greater adverse impacts on our tribe and our casino. To document those impacts, Colusa commissioned an independent study by Alan Meister and Clyde Barrow, two of the country's leading experts on the tribal gaming industry, and gave them access to actual data about the Colusa Casino's revenues, market area and patrons. This study projects an immediate decline in gross casino revenues of 39 percent when the Enterprise Casino opens, and a 55 percent decline in gross revenues when the Enterprise Casino reaches full operational capacity 2 years later. As a result, the Colusa Casino's EBITDA would decline by 65 percent when the Enterprise Casino opens, and by 77 percent when that casino reaches full operational capacity 2 years later. Further, the Colusa Casino's workforce would shrink by 35 percent in conjunction with the opening of the Enterprise Casino, and by 50 percent after 2 years. Nathan Associates Inc. & Pyramid Associates, LLC, *Economic Impacts of the Proposed Enterprise Rancheria Casino on the Colusa Indian Community and Colusa Casino Resort* (2013) ("Meister & Barrow").

The impact on Colusa's tribal government and the vital programs and services it provides to tribal members would be even more catastrophic, because the tribal government derives 85 percent of its non-grant, non-contract revenue from the Colusa Casino. Upon opening of the Enterprise Casino, Colusa's tribal government is projected to experience a 77 percent decline in revenues available for discretionary expenditures, and a 90 percent decline by 2 years later. Meister & Barrow. In short, approving a compact for an Enterprise Casino in Yuba County would virtually assure the impoverishment of the Colusa Indian Community, in order to enrich the Chicago gaming developer backing Enterprise's move from its existing gaming-eligible trust land base to a distant location with which Enterprise never has had a historical connection.

Meister and Barrow demonstrated that hundreds of our gaming and governmental employees will lose their jobs, Colusa County would lose hundreds of thousands of much-needed dollars every year, and our tribal citizens will lose many of the tribal programs and benefits that are needed to overcome the legacy of generations of poverty and deprivation. We are informed that a confidential study produced for California's Governor confirms that the proposed Enterprise Casino would have ten times more adverse impact on our casino than estimated in the Enterprise EIS.

Federal agencies have a duty in general to be skeptical of the claims of the beneficiaries and proponents of requested Federal decisions, and DOI has a fiduciary responsibility to all tribes to consider the adverse effects of its actions on them. Despite the Department's promise to apply "heavy scrutiny" to off-reservation applications, and that it would not approve off-reservation gaming that was "likely to [cause] a detrimental impact" on another tribe, however, it has relied upon the self-serving and unsupported claims of the project proponent to approve a project that would be exceptionally detrimental to surrounding tribes, while hiding behind an arbitrary 25-mile line to avoid consulting with those very same tribes.

The primary tool for analyzing the impacts of taking a parcel into trust for gaming purposes, like most major Federal actions, is the National Environmental Policy Act ("NEPA"). NEPA requires that a Federal agency take a "hard look" at the environmental impacts of its actions. Those environmental impacts include socioeconomic impacts. In addition, section 20 of IGRA and the regulations governing acquisition of land in trust for Indian tribes, 25 CFR parts 151 and 292, require analysis of the economic impacts. While NEPA regulations permit a project proponent to fund the environmental impact statement ("EIS"), they require that the Federal agency deciding whether to approve the project exercise oversight and exercise its independent judgment over preparation of the EIS. 40 CFR δ 1506.5. A Federal agency is required to "exercise a degree of skepticism in dealing with self-serving statements from a prime beneficiary of the project." *Simmons* v. *U.S. Army Corps of Eng'rs,* 120 F.3d 664, 666 (7th Cir.1997).

DOI did not exercise *any* skepticism with regard to the EIS paid for by YCE. YCE paid for the lawyers and environmental consultants to draft an application and a NEPA environmental assessment ("EA") on behalf of Enterprise, which only cursorily studied the environmental impacts of a casino on YCE's land near Marysville, CA. In 2005, BIA decided to require an EIS, which is longer than an EA. The same environmental consultant that produced the EA added an illusory alternative of constructing a casino on Enterprise's existing reservation to the EA as part of converting it into an EIS, but did not consider as an alternative putting into Federal trust for gaming a parcel of land in Butte County that Enterprise owns and is zoned for a hotel. Also, several of the studies underpinning the EIS were not updated from the EA stage. As part of its contract, the environmental consultant producing the EIS also had a contract to obtain the permits necessary for construction of the casino once DOI had acquired the land in trust, giving it a financial incentive to ensure that the casino was approved, rather than act as a neutral analyst for DOI.

In order to ensure that its preferred alternative casino was approved, the YCE-funded EIS "contrive[d] a purpose so slender as to define competing 'reasonable alternatives' out of consideration (and even out of existence)." *Simmons* v. *U.S. Army Corps of Eng'rs,* 120 F.3d 664, 669 (7th Cir.1997). The Council on Environmental Quality's ("CEQ's") regulations require that an EIS "shall briefly specify the underlying purpose and need to which the agency is responding in proposing the alternatives including the proposed action." 40 CFR § 1502.13. "[T]he statutory objectives of the project serve as a guide by which to determine the reasonableness of objectives outlined in an FEIS." *Westlands Water Dist.* v. *U.S. Dep't of Interior,* 376 F.3d 853, 866 (9th Cir.2004). As admitted by DOI in both the 2011 and 2012 RODs, Congress in IGRA intended confine tribal casinos to pre-1988 Indian Lands with extremely limited exceptions. 25 U.S.C. § 2719; 2011 ROD at 60.

Nonetheless, the Department approved an EIS that disregarded that important Congressional policy, and aimed solely at revenue maximization by a Class III casino, guaranteeing that only the largest Las Vegas-style casino in the best location possible would fulfill that purpose and need. EIS at 1–2 & 1–8. Thus, the two non-gaming alternatives were rejected because they did not include Class III gaming or produce enough revenue. The purpose and need was further narrowed to require the presence of YCE as Enterprise's gaming developer and manager (because it already owned the land that it would sell to Enterprise at an inflated price). *Id.* at 1–9. The EIS considered the alternative of a modest casino on Enterprise No. 1, but found that while it would produce a profit, it would produce far less than at the YCE site, and was thus rejected it would not produce as much income—income derived from cannibalizing other tribal governments' casino businesses. EIS at 2–39.

The report's authors, retained by YCE, speculated that it was "possible . . . that YCE would decline to enter into the agreement due to the changed circumstances and decreased potential revenues likely to result from Alternative D," the on-reservation casino. EIS at 2–41. Having been retained by YCE, the environmental consultant knew that the "changed circumstances" were that Enterprise would not need to purchase YCE's land or employ it as its developer/manager.

Indicative of its inattention to detail, the Department repeatedly misidentified the land owned by YCE that it proposed to take into trust for Enterprise. The YCE-funded EIS, the 2011 letter to Governor Brown, his 2012 concurrence in the acquisition of the YCE parcel, Assistant Secretary Washburn's decision to take the land into trust, and the **Federal Register** notice announcing that decision, among other documents described the land as totaling 40 acres. *E.g.,* 77 Fed. Reg. 71612 (2012). Many of the same documents, however, as well as the policy of title insurance proposed to be issued to the United States, included legal descriptions of a parcel of approximately 82.65 acres. Baker-Williams Engineering Group Letter to George Forman (January 2, 2013). DOI later issued a "correction" of the legal description and parcel number to reduce the land taken into trust to 40 acres. 78 Fed. Reg. 114 (2013). DOI's own regulations require that it closely examine title to proposed trust acquisition. 25 CFR part 151.13; 2002 Enterprise Application at 9 ("The land description in the deed and title evidence must be identical"). DOI guidance, which effectively has the force of law, requires that the Office of Indian Gaming "will review the description to verify that the description accurately describes the subject property, and that it is consistent throughout the application." Fee-to-Trust Handbook at 65 (2011).

In addition to not adequately examining the land itself or the impacts of acquiring it for Enterprise, the Department erred in finding that Enterprise *needed* YCE's land. The Enterprise Rancheria originally consisted of two 40-acre parcels in Butte County that were purchased in 1915. In 1964, tribal members agreed to sell one of the parcels of land, Enterprise No. 2, to the State of California for inundation by Lake Oroville. The other parcel, Enterprise No. 1, over which the tribal government of the Enterprise Rancheria has jurisdiction, remains in trust. *Robert Edwards* v. *Pacific Regional Director, Bureau of Indian Affairs,* 45 IBIA 42 (2007). Having been in trust prior to October 17, 1988, Enterprise No. 1 constitutes "Indian Lands" that are eligible for gaming under IGRA.

DOI's regulations require that the Department find that a tribe has a need for land, not just the desire for it. 25 CFR part 151.10(b); 2012 ROD at 44. Nor could DOI find such a need. According to the EIS funded by Enterprise's own gaming developer, a casino on its existing reservation, Enterprise No. 1, could turn a profit from which the tribe's several hundred members entitled to full benefits would receive. *E.g.,* EIS at 4.7–17 to 4.7–28; Appendix M at 130.

Nonetheless, the 2012 Record of Decision approving the application to have the YCE parcel taken into trust found that Enterprise needed more land. 2012 ROD at 44. Assistant Secretary Echo Hawk the year before had found that development of Enterprise No. 1 would be "exceedingly difficult" and would "result in minimal or no revenue for the tribe." 2011 ROD at 47. The report on economic impacts, however, found that an on-reservation casino would have total annual revenues of nearly $20,000,000. Appendix M at 130; EIS at 2.47. While that pales in comparison to an estimated total revenue at the YCE parcel of $160,000,000, it is not "minimal" revenue. Moreover, the ROD failed to consider the development potential of Enterprise-owned fee land in Butte County, much closer to Enterprise's existing gaming-eligible trust land base.

Although the costs of construction of an on-reservation casino were estimated to be higher in proportion to total revenues—based solely on YCE's figures and without explanation—the cost of debt and revenue sharing with its developer and local communities—such as the $5,000,000 annual payment in lieu of property taxes to the County of Yuba—would not be present. *Memorandum of Understanding between the Estom Yumeka Maidu Tribe, Enterprise Rancheria and the County of Yuba* (December 17, 2002); Appendix M at 46. The estimated costs to Enterprise of an off-reservation casino were $150,000,000 in 2006. *Id.* 11. For the sake of "accuracy," however, GMA excluded from that figure the cost of Enterprise purchasing the casino site from YCE at the above-market price of $7,000,000 or the costs and 13 percent interest Enterprise agreed to pay for the up to $85,000,000 projected cost in 2002 (to be borrowed from YCE and other lenders to finance its fee-to-trust application, purchase of YCE's land, pay for construction, and a management fee of 30 percent of the *net* revenues of the off-reservation casino). *E.g.,* 2002 Enterprise Application at 16, 99 & 107. Since Enterprise already beneficially owned its existing reservation, there would be no cost to purchase land for an on-reservation casino.

Moreover, Enterprise already owns more than 80 acres of land in fee-simple in Butte County, which is more than twice the size of Enterprise No. 2, which it agreed to sell to California in 1964. Enterprise Properties in Context; *see also, http://goo.gl/maps/LhUq7.* Since the Enterprise tribal government reconstituted itself in 1994 it has received millions of dollars in Federal funding to support government programs, including funding to acquire land for tribal housing. *E.g.,* 62 Fed. Reg. 52348 (1997) (notice of award of $2.3 Million to Enterprise for Indian housing). It also has received millions of dollars from the Revenue Sharing Trust Fund established under California's 1999 Class III gaming compacts. Despite its claims to be a Yuba County tribe, it has never purchased land in Yuba County. North State Research & Consulting Services, Research Report (March 21, 2013) (listing Enterprise Rancheria properties in the public records of Butte County); North State Research & Consulting Services, Research Report (April 10, 2013) (finding no Enterprise Rancheria properties in the public records of Yuba or Sutter Counties).

Notably, Enterprise's lands include a 63-acre parcel outside of Oroville, 2009 Enterprise Application at 4, and a 16-acre parcel, which already includes a hotel, between Enterprise No. 1 and the former Enterprise No. 2. Research Report (March 21, 2013). It also owns the office building in Oroville housing the tribal government's office, and several residential properties in Oroville. *Id.* Enterprise has never sought to have any of those properties it owns in Butte County taken into trust by DOI. 2009 Enterprise Application at 4. The only trust land it is interested in is the Yuba County property owned by its casino backer, YCE.

Enterprise No. 1 may not be ideal for gaming, but scores of other California Indian tribes find themselves in a similar or worse situation with either land that could not support a casino or without land at all. Such tribes, such as Colusa, have incurred heavy debt burdens to finance casinos on their less-than-ideal lands and to develop a customer base outside of their small, local communities. Some of those tribes with remote reservations, such as Santa Ysabel, which recently unsuccessfully attempted to declare bankruptcy, have come close to failing, but only Enterprise has been allowed by DOI to make a developer-backed foray into other tribes' traditional territories for the sole purpose of gaining access to more lucrative markets, deliberately cannibalizing the marginal markets of other tribes in the process. If a developer's willingness to finance a casino and a tribe's desire for greater profit is the standard by which to judge section 20 two-part determinations, there are scores of California tribes just as, or more deserving than Enterprise of being allowed to move to more lucrative locations; this would include some of the State's largest tribes.

In both northern and southern California, there are numerous tribes—large and small—with small, remote and/or rugged gaming-eligible trust land bases. Those tribes include, but are not limited to, the Covelo Indian Community (Mendocino County), the Quartz Valley Rancheria (Siskiyou County), the Cold Springs Rancheria (Fresno County), Grindstone Rancheria (Glenn County), Cortina Rancheria (Colusa County), Ramona Reservation (Riverside County), Santa Rosa Reservation (Riverside County), Manzanita Reservation (San Diego County), Los Coyotes Reservation (San Diego County), Ewiiaapaayp Reservation (San Diego County), Jamul Reservation (San Diego County), La Jolla Reservation (San Diego County), Hoopa Valley Reservation (Humboldt County), Yurok Reservation (Humboldt and Del Norte Counties), Lower Lake Rancheria (Lake County), El Em (Sulphur Bank) Rancheria (Lake County), Ft. Bidwell Reservation (Modoc County), Benton Paiute Reservation (Inyo County), Inaja-Cosmit Reservation (San Diego County), Bridgeport Indian Colony (Alpine County), Big Sandy Rancheria (Madera County), Table Mountain Rancheria (Fresno County), Bear River Rancheria (Humboldt County), Mooretown Rancheria (Butte County), Cahuilla Reservation (Riverside County), Chemehuevi Reservation), Berry Creek Rancheria (Butte County), and San Pasqual Reservation, among others. In addition, a number of tribes that were unterminated under the Tillie Hardwick decision still do not have trust lands, but are making efforts to acquire such lands in the vicinity of their former lands (e.g., Chico Rancheria, Cloverdale Rancheria, Scotts Valley Rancheria).

In approving off-reservation gaming by Enterprise, DOI relied upon the fiction that the YCE parcel is within the tribe's traditional territory and that it was "strongly supported" by the local community. 2011 ROD at 63–64. Although Enterprise, a Maidu tribe, claims that Yuba and Sutter Counties are its aboriginal territory, that claim is easily debunked by reviewing the authoritative treatises on the subject of California Indian tribes. Marcos Guerrero, Affidavit (December 24, 2012). It has no more claim to land in Yuba County than its fellow Butte County Maidu tribes, Mooretown and Berry Creek Rancherias, whose reservations are near Enterprise No. 1. *See http://goo.gl/maps/LhUq7.* Enterprise tacitly admitted that fact in its application for the two-part determination in which it noted that it provides services in Yuba and Sutter Counties in cooperation with the other two Maidu tribes in Butte County. 2009 Enterprise Application at 5. Despite the assertions of historic ties to Yuba County, only about one-half dozen tribal members of any class lived in Yuba County in 2002–2009. *Id.* at 3; 2002 Enterprise Application at 3 (approximately 10 percent of its 500 members lived in Yuba and Sutter Counties).

The sole evidence for Enterprise's claims to aboriginal territory in Yuba County is a single decision by the California Native American Heritage Commission, which found Enterprise to be a most likely descendant of specific remains found during excavation for a levee on the Feather River. That finding was contested by other Feather River Tribes. The fact that the Army Corps of Engineers is participating in that project allowed Enterprise to claim that both the State and Federal governments support its claims. 2012 ROD at 46. At some point, the claim was vastly expanded from a portion of the bank of the Feather River to include all of Yuba and Sutter Counties without any explanation. *See* 2009 Application at 13; 2011 ROD at 46; *But see,* Guerrero Affidavit.

Although backed by several local governments that entered into potentially lucrative side agreements with Enterprise, the project was rejected by the voters of Yuba County in a 2005 ballot initiative by a clearer margin than many Presidential elections. Yuba County Board of Supervisors' Letter to BIA (March 17, 2009). The voters had earlier approved the use of the land for a racetrack, a very different and periodic land use that would have been subject to local control and taxation. Crucially, however, it would not have been as lucrative for YCE. Notwithstanding popular opposition, DOI found strong local support for the casino based on the actions of local elected officials, especially the Yuba County Supervisors, who had acted prior to the ballot initiative. 2011 ROD at 47.

In order to gain the support of DOI and the State of California, Enterprise has relied upon ambiguity to make it appear that a Yuba County casino will benefit a large number of impoverished local tribal members. While their poverty is probably, and lamentably, real, the direct benefits of a casino will not flow to that many tribal members. When Enterprise first organized as a tribe in 1994, its General Council—all voting members of the tribe—amounted to fewer than 20 people. Letter from Enterprise Rancheria to BIA (1994). Membership was initially limited to the direct descendants of the occupants of Enterprise Nos. 1 and 2, and thus necessarily originated in Butte County. Enterprise adopted a constitution to admit a literal second class of citizens: persons who are not lineally descended from the original occupants of Enterprise Nos. 1 and 2, but who could demonstrate Indian descent from anywhere in the Feather River drainage. By calling them "members," the tribe thus enables them to access Federal programs and services available to Indians. However, this second class of members cannot vote, cannot hold tribal office, and *are not eligible to receive any tribal benefits*—such as *per capita* distributions of casino revenues. Thus, the huge casino that Enterprise proposes to build actually will benefit far fewer individuals than Enterprise has claimed. Enterprise Constitution, Article III, Membership.

Colusa does not oppose any other tribe receiving the benefits of tribal government gaming. Our Tribe is a willing contributor to the California Indian Gaming Special Distribution Fund and Revenue Sharing Trust Fund, from which non-gaming tribes, such as the Enterprise and North Fork Rancherias, receive $1.1 million per year in completely unrestricted funds. If Enterprise were seeking to conduct Class III gaming on or close to its existing gaming-eligible trust lands, we would not oppose it. Similarly, we strongly support the Department of the Interior ("DOI") accepting land into Federal trust for tribes whose original trust lands were taken—not voluntarily sold—or lost through termination, or if a tribe needs more land for housing, cultural purposes or even economic development if that development would not impoverish our own tribe. In most cases, that sort of trust land acquisition is unlikely to have any significant impact on other tribes, unless the newly acquired land is within another tribe's traditional territory.

Our opposition to DOI's off-reservation gaming acquisitions is not based on a lack of sympathy for the history of other Indian tribes that must continue to deal with the legacy of genocide, displacement and failed attempts at forced assimilation that characterized so much of United States and California's history. The fact is that every Indian tribe—ours included—has to deal with that legacy every day. We oppose acquisition of off-reservation land in trust for gaming purposes for Enterprise because if historic mistreatment of Indian tribes and their members justifies allowing Enterprise to leapfrog its fellow tribes to build a casino closer to the nearest major market than neighboring tribes, then that justification applies equally to every other tribe that is not located near either a major highway and/or a large city. That would include most tribes in the country—including our own tribe.

But that is not what Congress had in mind when it enacted the Indian Gaming Regulatory Act ("IGRA") in 1988. Nor is it what the people of California voted for in 1998 when they passed Proposition 5 and again in 2000 when they passed Proposition 1a. Voters nationwide and within California do not support "reservation-shopping" by tribes. If Congress or the voters of the State of California believed that would be the outcome, neither IGRA nor the California Propositions that enabled tribal government gaming would have passed. Moreover, once tribes become viewed by the public as nothing more than fronts for casino developers, the public likely will cease to view tribes as governments exercising authority over territory, with devastating consequences for all tribes.

We oppose the DOI's current off-reservation gaming policy because it threatens to destroy much of the progress that our tribe and others have made. Our reservation is located in rural Colusa County. We started in gaming with a modest high-stakes bingo hall 30 years ago, and we slowly grew our modest casino as revenues and the market permitted. Our casino generates most of the revenues that our tribe has used to provide programs and services to our members that no other unit of government had been providing—services such as medical care, education, nutrition, public safety, environmental protection, recreation and other services. We also have used—and pledged—casino revenues to diversify our tribal economy.

As the result of our casino revenues and the economic development it has supported, our tribe is now one of the largest employers in Colusa County, and our tribe is an important contributor both to local governments in Colusa County and to the economy of the area as a whole. The development of our tribe's economy also has resulted in our tribe becoming a respected agricultural business locally and potentially globally. All of that stands to be lost due to a Federal agency's failure to apply sufficient skepticism to the claims of a gaming developer who stands to make tens of millions of dollars annually from tribal gaming and hundreds of millions over the 7 years of his development and management contracts with Enterprise.

We don't think IGRA needs to be changed. We do think that the DOI and BIA need to change the way two-part determinations are being made. Otherwise, all that we—and other tribes in our area—have worked so hard and long to accomplish will be lost.

Thank you for the opportunity to share my Tribe's views with the subcommittee.

———

Mr. YOUNG. Thank you, Hazel. I have been reading your written statement. It will be in the record. There are a lot of good things in there. Some of it was a little legalese for me, but it is pretty good. So, thank you.

Ms. LONGMIRE. Thank you.

Mr. YOUNG. Doctor.

STATEMENT OF ALEXANDER SKIBINE, PROFESSOR, UNIVERSITY OF UTAH

Mr. SKIBINE. Thank you, Mr. Chairman, members of the subcommittee. Good afternoon, and thank you for allowing me to testify today on this important matter.

I was deputy counsel here, for Indian Affairs, between 1980 and 1990. I was the deputy to Frank Ducheneaux. And I can confirm, Mr. Chairman, that he is completely responsible for any deficiency in the language as it currently exists in section 20.

[Laughter.]

Mr. SKIBINE. Having said that, I also want to emphasize that I agree with you, that no one wants to authorize another Indian casino just to see a previous one go out of business. It is something that we should be very careful about.

And, finally, I want to join Chairwoman Longmire in her assessment that I do not think that IGRA should be amended, or need to be amended.

Having blamed Frank for the language, in effect, it is my position that the section has worked well, so far. Since 1988 there have been 14 denials and 15 approvals. Out of those 15 approvals, 5 were vetoed by the State Governor, and one, the last one, in Menomonie, is still pending. So, basically, the tribes are batting 50 percent.

Under IGRA, the Secretary can only find that gaming will be beneficial to the tribe and not detrimental to the surrounding community, after consultation with local officials, which include officials from other Indian tribes. Perhaps the most salient features contained in the section are that the Governor of the State has to concur to the two-part determination. And, more importantly, the Governor can disagree for any reason.

Concerning your questions to the Assistant Secretary, in effect there has been a lot of litigation in State court concerning the authority of the Governors to agree or disagree under local State law. And, in effect, the legislature can constrain his authority—the State legislature can, if they want to.

Mr. YOUNG. Doctor, are you saying that the Governor isn't the final say in this? They can override him?

Mr. SKIBINE. The legislature can basically impose requirements on the Governor. As a matter of fact, there is one litigation where the legislature has to ratify the Governor's concurrence.

Mr. YOUNG. And—how many times has the legislature turned the Governor down?

Mr. SKIBINE. I don't have that information.

Mr. YOUNG. OK, we will get that.

Mr. SKIBINE. All right. In addition, there are many additional safeguards that have been imposed by the executive branch. The 2008 regulations required the tribes to present evidence of significant historical connections to the land. In addition, the distance of the land from the tribal headquarters has to be taken into consideration. Finally, the tribe has to show how the relationship between the tribe and the non-Indian community will be benefited.

But before the land can actually be transferred into trust, in effect, the tribe also has to go through the requirements of Section 5 of the IRA. And, the regulations were implemented in 1995 and they contain 11 criteria that have to be evaluated: among others, impact on the local tax roles; the potential jurisdictional problems; and the regulation also provide that greater scrutiny has to be given to the concerns of local officials the further their lands are from the existing reservation. So, under the IRA, in effect, distance is a factor and an important factor.

Finally, each determination can be subject to exacting judicial scrutiny. Under the APA the decision cannot be arbitrary or capricious. Every relevant factor has to be considered by the Secretary. Also, after the *Carcieri* case, in order to be eligible under the IRA, the tribe has to be under Federal jurisdiction as of 1934.

Finally, under the recent *Patchak* decision, the Quiet Title Act no longer protects such trust acquisition from being challenged by almost anyone with a stake in the outcome.

So, in conclusion, you know, I think that the standards have worked well. Can it need some tweaking? Probably. It is true that there is no definition of what is detrimental to surrounding community. And it is also true that perhaps there should be more emphasis on how the creation of a new Indian casino will endanger existing casinos in the areas.

But I think that this should be done through regulations, instead of legislation at this point. Because my experience is that, any legislation has to pass the House and then go to the Senate. And it seems that if you are going to amend IGRA, the chances of this being just a tweaking, is remote. Once it gets to the Senate, who knows what they will be able to do with this legislation. Thank you, Mr. Chairman.

[The prepared statement of Mr. Skibine follows:]

PREPARED STATEMENT OF ALEXANDER SKIBINE,[1] PROFESSOR, UNIVERSITY OF UTAH

Mr. Chairman, members of the subcommittee, thank you for inviting to testify on these important matters. My statement today is going to focus on Executive decisions to authorize gaming on off-reservation land acquired into trust after 1988. More precisely, my comments will address those Executive decisions made pursuant to the two-part determination set out in section (b)(1)(A) of the Indian Gaming Regulatory Act of 1988, 25 U.S.C. 2719(b)(1)(A). These are the decisions which require concurrence by a State Governor.

Under IGRA's section 20, gaming is prohibited on lands acquired by the Secretary of the Interior after October 17, 1988, unless such lands are located within or contiguous to the boundaries of an Indian reservation as of that date. The law contains 4 exceptions to this prohibition. Under the so-called "two-part determination" exception, gaming is allowed on off reservation land if the Secretary determines, after consultation with appropriate state and local officials, including officials of nearby Indian tribes, that gaming at that location would be in the best interest of the tribe

[1] S.J. Quinney Professor of Law, University of Utah S.J. Quinney College of Law.

46

and its members and would not be detrimental to the surrounding community. In addition, the Governor of the affected State has to concur with this determination.

There is almost no legislative history concerning the enactment of section 20. The concept of a restriction on off reservation gaming seemed to have first surfaced in a bill introduced by Congressman Bereuter of Nebraska in 1985, (H.R. 3130, 99th Congress.) The idea behind that bill was eventually incorporated by the Senate Select Committee on Indian Affairs when it reported out of committee an amended version of H.R. 1920, the gaming bill which had passed the House of Representatives on April 21, 1986. Although H.R. 1920 never passed the Senate, its main components, including the section which restricted gaming on lands acquired outside Indian reservations were incorporated in S. 555, the Indian gaming bill which eventually passed the Congress and was signed by the President.[2]

WHAT THE RECORD SHOWS

Since 1988, the Secretary has disapproved 14 two-part determinations, 12 of these disapprovals were made in or after 2008, including one in 2011.

Since 1988, the Secretary has approved 15 two-part determinations, 5 of which were approved in 2011 or thereafter. Of these 15 approvals, 5 were vetoed by State Governors, 1 has not been acted upon yet.

Of the five decisions made since 2011, four were approvals, one was a disapproval.

Finally, it is my understanding that there are currently 10 applications involving two-part determinations still pending at the Department.

One of the more controversial aspect of off reservation gaming is that it may occur at a location far from a tribe's reservation. Of the more recent approvals the record indicates the following:

—Kaw Nation (Oklahoma): 21 miles from former reservation, 41 miles from tribal headquarters.
—Keweenaw Bay Indian Community (Michigan): 70 miles from reservation and tribal headquarters. (Governor vetoed).
—Enterprise Rancheria (Ca.): 36 miles from the tribal headquarters.
—North Fork Rancheria (Ca.): 36 miles from headquarters.
—Menominee Indian Tribe of Wisconsin: 160 miles from tribe's reservation.

Of the one recent disapproval, the record indicates that the proposed land was 293 miles from the Pueblo of Jemez (New Mexico).

The purpose of my testimony today is to show that overall, there are more than enough safeguards currently in place to guarantee that the Secretary's decisions to allow gaming on off reservation lands acquired after 1988 will continue to be made rationally and fairly and that the Secretary's discretion will not be abused. These safeguards have been imposed by all three branches of the government.

A. Legislatively Imposed Requirements

IGRA contains several important requirements restricting off reservation gaming. The most important one is the one requiring the Governor of the State to concur with the Secretary's two part determination. As mentioned above, that requirement has already resulted in five vetoes by State Governors. A salient feature of that requirement is that there does not seem to be any federally imposed standards on the State Governors. This means that a State Governor may refuse to concur with a Secretary's determination for just about any reason.

Another important requirement is that the two-part determination can only be made after consultation with State and local officials. Furthermore, gaming on such newly acquired lands cannot be "detrimental" to the surrounding communities, although the act does not further define what "detrimental" means in this context.

Another important IGRA restriction is that gaming under the act is only allowed on Indian lands and the definition of Indian lands indicates that for trust or restricted lands located off Indian reservations, the Indian tribe has to be exercising "governmental power" before such lands can be considered Indian lands under IGRA. This requirement seemed to have played a crucial role in disapproving the application of the Pueblo of Jemez.

Before taking land into trust, the Secretary also has to comply with the requirements of NEPA. Among other things, this means that the Secretary has to give adequate consideration to a reasonable range of alternative sites for the proposed gaming establishments, and has to take a "hard look" at the environmental impacts of the proposed action.

---

[2]For an in depth discussion of the legislative history of IGRA, see Robert N. Clinton, *Enactment of the Indian Gaming Regulatory Act of 1988: The Return of the Buffalo to Indian Country or Another Federal Usurpation of Tribal Sovereignty*, 42 Ariz. St. L. J. 17 (2010).

B. Executive Branch's Safeguards: The 2008 and 1995 Regulations

In 2008, 20 years after enactment of IGRA, the Interior Department published detailed regulations providing further guidance and direction for the implementation of this section. Subpart C, sections 292.13 to 292.24 concerns the two-part determination exception. These regulations contain additional factors a tribe has to meet in order for the land to qualify under that exception.

For instance, in order to assist the Secretary in determining whether the proposed gaming will be in the best interest of the tribe and its members, the tribe must present "evidence of significant historical connections to the land." 292.17(i). The tribe must also provide the "distance of the land from the location where the tribe maintains core governmental functions" (g). In addition, the tribal application must describe the "projected benefits to the relationship between the tribe and non-Indian communities." (e). In reality, this last criteria has resulted in no land acquisition being transferred into trust without the support of the surrounding community.[3]

In addition to comply with the requirements of IGRA for gaming purposes, before land can actually be taken into trust, a tribe also has to also comply with the requirements of the Indian Reorganization Act of 1934 (IRA). Although the IRA does not contain much of a standard, authorizing the Secretary in his discretion to acquire land within or without existing Indian reservations for the purpose of providing land for Indians, the Secretary adopted new regulations in 1995 which for the first time made a distinction between on and off reservation land acquisition and further restricted the discretion previously enjoyed by the Secretary under the act.[4]

The 1995 regulations contain 11 criteria for taking land into trust. Seven are applicable to all tribal land acquisitions and an additional four are applicable only for off reservation acquisitions. Some of the criteria are hard to reconcile with the trust doctrine and the original purpose of the IRA which was to stop the allotment process and allow Indians to re-acquire some of the land base that had been lost as a result of allotment.[5] For instance under criteria (e) the Secretary has to consider the impact the acquisition will have on the tax rolls of the State and its political subdivisions. Under criteria (f), the Secretary has to consider the jurisdictional problems and potential land use conflicts which may arise from the proposed land acquisition. Finally, for off reservation acquisitions, under criteria (b) the secretary has to give greater scrutiny to the tribe's justification of anticipated benefits and to the concerns raised by state and local officials, the further the lands are from the reservation. These criteria were fatal to at least one proposed land acquisition even though the tribe involved (St. Regis Mohawk) had already successfully navigated all the requirements of IGRA's two-part determination.

To tribal advocates, the three criteria just mentioned above are hard to justify especially when one consider how comparatively easy it is to take land out of trust status. As recently noted by Professor Frank Pommersheim, there is currently still more Indian land going out of trust than land being put into trust throughout Indian country.[6]

C. Judicially Imposed Requirements

Any overreaching by the Department of the Interior can be adequately controlled by the Federal courts. The recent litigation involving North Fork Rancheria of Mono Indians provides a good example of how thorough judicial review can be under the Administrative Procedure Act (APA).[7] Set forth below is a roadmap the Department has to successfully navigate in order to get the proposed land into trust:

First, under the APA any agency decision can be set aside if it is arbitrary and capricious, an abuse of discretion, or otherwise not in accordance with law. Under that standard, the court has to make sure that the agency has "examined the relevant data and articulated a satisfactory explanation for its action including a rational connection between the facts found and the choice made."[8] In other words,

---

[3] Although there seemed to have been one pre-2008 approval (Siletz Tribe of Oregon in 1992) that did not have the support of the local community, the State Governor quickly vetoed the two-part determination by refusing to concur with the Secretary's decision.

[4] For a comprehensive treatment of the fee to trust process, see Frank Pommersheim, *Land into Trust: An Inquiry Into Law, Policy, and History,* 49 Idaho L. Rev. 519 (2013).

[5] It has been estimated that Indian tribes had control of about 138 million acres at the close of the treaty period in 1871. It has been estimated that by 1934, the tribal land base had shrunk to 48 million acres, a 90 million acres loss. See Readjustment of Indian Affairs: Hearings on H.R. 7902, House Committee on Indian Affairs, 73d Cong.2d Sess. 16 (1934).

[6] See Pommersheim *supra,* at note 4.

[7] *Stand Up for California* v. *North Fork Rancheria,* 919 F.Supp.2d 51 (2013).

[8] *Motor Vehicle* v. *State Farm,* 463 U.S. 29, 43 (1983).

the agency action has to be the product of reasoned decisionmaking. The agency has to consider every important aspect of the problem, and cannot "offer an explanation for its decision that runs counter to the evidence, or is so implausible that it could not be ascribed to a difference in view or the product of agency expertise."[9]

Second, under *Carcieri* v. *Salazar,* 555 U.S. 279 (2009), the Secretary can only obtain land into trust under the 1934 Indian Reorganization Act for federally recognized Indian tribes that were "under Federal jurisdiction" in 1934. According to the BIA's own statement "whether a tribe was under Federal jurisdiction in 1934 requires a fact-intensive analysis of the history of interactions between that tribe and the United States."

Third, the courts will scrutinize whether the Secretary adequately considered the impacts of the proposed gaming on the surrounding community. In the *North Fork* decision for instance, the court went into a detailed examination of the following: 1. Problem gambling, 2. Crime, 3. Environmental and economic impacts, 4. Effects on other local Indian tribes.

Finally, under the recent *Patchak* Supreme Court decision,[10] the Quiet Title Act (QTA) no longer prevents almost anyone impacted by the decision to challenge a fee to trust transfer to an Indian tribe even after the transfer of trust title to the United States has already taken place.

CONCLUSION

It seems that there are plenty of existing obstacles an Indian tribe has to surmount before it can actually acquire off reservation land for gaming purposes. Regulations implementing both IGRA and the IRA contain many requirements obligating the Secretary to take into account the concerns of both the non-Indian community and other Indian tribes, as well as the distance of the lands to be acquired from the existing reservation or tribal headquarters. Although this distance factor is not included in either the language of the IRA or IGRA, I am not opposed to it being "a" factor. However for the following reasons, I do not think it should be the determinative factor.

First, it cannot be forgotten that many Indian tribes were removed from their traditional territories.[11] Furthermore, tribal economic development was never considered during the removal era. Quite the opposite: tribes were removed to far-away places to facilitate non-Indian economic activities.

Second, it has to be understood that when it comes to economic development, Indian tribes are not just acting as businesses trying to make a quick buck. They are in the process of raising governmental revenues because they lack the tax base on their existing reservations.[12] To a large degree, the U.S. Supreme Court is responsible for this state of affairs as it has severely curtail the tribes' power to tax non-members,[13] while at the same time allowing the States more and more taxing power within the reservations.[14]

Third, it cannot be ignored that these off reservation land acquisitions benefit much more than just the gaming Indian tribe. In many of these off reservation acquisitions, tribes have committed to make significant financial contributions to the budgets of local governments. In addition, in all of these gaming operations, most of the casino workforce consists of non-tribal members. Furthermore, these gaming establishments have and will continue to make very positive contributions to the local economy.

Finally, the era when Indians were supposed to be confined to reservations is long gone, and the idea that tribal economic development should solely be a reservation based activity is no longer in fashion.[15] As a matter of fact, the latest census reveals that far more Indians reside outside Indian reservations than within them. The whole concept of sovereignty as being solely geographically or territorially based has been significantly eroded and has evolved to a more malleable concept recognizing the interrelationship between various sovereign actors.[16] It is this interrelationship

---

[9] *Id.,* at 43, 52.

[10] *Match-E-Be-Nash-She-Wish Band of Potawatomi Indians* v. *Patchak,* 132 S. Ct. 2199 (2012).

[11] The 2005 Edition of Cohen's Handbook of Federal Indian law noted that "by 1850, the majority of Indian tribes had been removed from the Eastern States. (at p. 54)

[12] See Matthew L.M. Fletcher, In Pursuit of economic Development as a Substitute for Reservation Tax Revenue, 80 N.D. L. Rev. 759 (2004).

[13] See *Atkinson Trading Co.* v. *Shirley,* 532 U.S. 645 (2001).

[14] See *Cotton Petroleum* v. *New Mexico,* 490 U.S. 163 (1989).

[15] See Alex Tallchief Skibine, *Tribal Sovereign Interests Beyond the Reservation Borders,* 12 Lewis & Clark L. Rev. 1003 (2008).

[16] See for instance, John Alan Cohan, *Sovereignty in a Postmodern World,* 18 Fla. J. Int'l L. 907 (2006), Helen Stacy, *Relational Sovereignty,* 55 Stan. L. Rev. 2029 (2003), Neil MacCormick,

between tribes and the surrounding local governments and communities that is being promoted and developed in these off reservation land acquisitions.

———

Mr. YOUNG. Doctor, I agree with you on the Senate part.

[Laughter.]

Mr. YOUNG. LaMalfa.

Mr. LAMALFA. Thank you, Mr. Chairman, for allowing me to move ahead a bit to get to the Floor. I appreciate that.

You know, in the area I represent in northern California there is, within about a 150-mile radius, there are already 7 gaming tribe sites in that area, 4 of which are especially approximate to Colusa nearby. So, asking Ms. Longmire, we have heard different numbers on what the impact would be of an additional off-reservation site there. And I think the other parties involved cite, did you say a number between 3 and 7 percent, and then your number was what, what figure upon your operation?

Ms. LONGMIRE. Our operation would have been affected at least by 77 percent. Well, if the casino Enterprise would open up, immediate decline in casino gross revenues would have been 39 percent. And 55 percent decline in gross revenues when Enterprise casino reaches full operation capacity in 2 years. As a result, the Colusa's EBITDA would decline by 65 percent when the Enterprise casino opens, and by 75 percent when that casino reaches full operational capacities 2 years later.

Mr. LAMALFA. So you hadn't counted upon this type of off-reservation operation coming near you, obviously, when you built your infrastructure the size the way you did. And you are making your business plan of what would you sustain in this area, what kind of income and traffic would you expect to your casino, you didn't have that anticipated, there would now be a new competition outside of this—the——

Ms. LONGMIRE. No, we didn't.

Mr. LAMALFA [continuing]. Present rules.

Ms. LONGMIRE. We did not. But the other casinos around us, even though there are some to the northeast of us, which is about 30—maybe a little over 35 miles, there is one north of us 45 minutes away, and then there is one south of us, probably maybe another 45 minutes——

Mr. LAMALFA. And even farther north about 80 miles or so, too.

Ms. LONGMIRE. Right.

Mr. LAMALFA. So—yes. But none of those went the off-reservation route.

Ms. LONGMIRE. No. And we have no problem with that.

Mr. LAMALFA. Yes.

Ms. LONGMIRE. And—but this, I think our biggest worry was that the land was actually put into trust. We thought that would never happen, because it is not their traditional territory. When that happened, we were really worried that we would lose, our tribe would actually be gone. It would.

Mr. LAMALFA. OK, thank you. Mr. Chairman, I wanted to propose that I think the representatives of BIA are not here any more today. But maybe, if I could ask your support, and Ranking Mem-

———

Beyond the Sovereign State, 56 Mod. L. Rev. 1 (1993), Allan R. Stein, *Frontiers of Jurisdiction: From Isolation to Connectedness,* 2001 U. Chi. Legal F. 373 (2001).

50

ber, as well, to invite Mr. Washburn and BIA members to this area of California to view firsthand the proximity and the effects upon this.

Because, again, the 25-mile rule doesn't seem to be very legitimate in this type of territory. This is flat geography, pretty much. And it is nothing to think of 25 miles. And in the process, here, you have two very disparate studies on what the impact is going to be. And if we are wrong on this, then it is going to be very detrimental to at least one tribe, and maybe four or more in an approximate area.

Mr. YOUNG. We will, I will, with you, and I hope the Ranking— we just ask them to visit your area, as long as you host it. My back history, I used to date a girl from Colusa before they had casinos. And she threw me out. That is one reason I am in Alaska.

[Laughter.]

Mr. YOUNG. But I know the area very well. But, no, we would be more than glad to do it.

That is what I said about this 25-mile area. I don't understand it. I mean, again, the market can only bear so much. And when you invest in something with the understanding that this is not going to happen again, and then someone jumps into an area that really doesn't have any right to it, that is why I told Washburn this. So, hopefully he will see the wisdom of being a little more realistic, and we will get into that later with the doctor here, but——

Mr. LAMALFA. OK. I would appreciate working with you on a letter on that.

Mr. YOUNG. Yes.

Mr. LAMALFA. And, you know, even auto dealers have territories.

Mr. YOUNG. That is right.

Mr. LAMALFA. And that makes business sense for them.

Mr. YOUNG. Right. So do drug dealers, but that is beside the point.

[Laughter.]

Mr. LAMALFA. Well, we will make sure you are safe in Colusa, if you decide to come. Thank you, Mr. Chairman.

Mr. YOUNG. Madam.

Mr. LAMALFA. Thank you, Ranking Member.

Mr. YOUNG. You have my permission to introduce anybody you want to.

Ms. HANABUSA. Thank you, Mr. Chair. First of all, I would like to do a shout-out to Mr. Sosa, who decided to stay after seeing me. He is the 2013 Hawaii High School Principal of the Year. He has come in all the way from Honolulu Kaiser High School.

[Applause.]

Ms. HANABUSA. Thank you for staying. Thank you, Mr. Chair.

My questions are for you, Professor. And the reason I am so curious is because what we are hearing so much about is a process that is not taking into account community input and implications of the economic implications, and so forth.

But in actuality, in your testimony, you have listed a battery of steps that can really slow this process down, beginning with the National Environmental Protection Act, beginning with an Administrative Procedures Act challenge, and, of course, recently the *Patchak* is the way I refer to that Supreme Court decision, which almost makes it really just an open field for people to go and challenge any kind of an administrative decision that is made.

So, given these three steps, which I believe are challenges that—one, definitely NEPA can be made prior to a decision, when you believe it is inadequate, and if they have accepted it, and the other two. Can you just quickly go through that process? And, from your experience, say how that can just give people another bite, or maybe two more bites of the apple.

Mr. SKIBINE. The process under the APA?

Ms. HANABUSA. Yes.

Mr. SKIBINE. Well, basically, anybody can challenge this, and the courts are going to give, what we call a hard-look review to everything that was done by the agency in order to support its decision.

So, that means that they have to look at every factor, the relevant factor, they have to address all the concerns. And they have to find, in effect, what amounts to substantial evidence in order to support their decision. And as a result, you know, it is a very involved process and this is why Kevin Washburn mentioned that his last decision was 53 pages. I have read through that decision, and it is extremely thorough.

And also, in my testimony, my written testimony, I mentioned the *North Fork* case. That was appealed to a district court. And you can see in there, this is another 53-page decision by the district court, where the judge basically went through every one of the steps to figure out that this was not arbitrary and capricious.

Ms. HANABUSA. And in addition to that, with the *Patchak* decision by the United States Supreme Court recently, what it does do is it gives almost anyone the opportunity to challenge a decision of taking lands into trust, as well, correct?

Mr. SKIBINE. That is right. That is right.

Ms. HANABUSA. And——

Mr. SKIBINE. And as a matter of fact, there is a case still pending, that may actually be your case, where the district court issued a decision and it is in litigation.

Ms. HANABUSA. And when you say it is your case, are you talking to Hazel?

Mr. SKIBINE. To Hazel Longmire. I think it is her tribe.

Ms. HANABUSA. Oh, yes.

Mr. SKIBINE. There is one case where, in effect, the court mentioned the *Patchak* decision. It is the *Cachil Dehe Band of Wintun Indians of the Colusa Indian Community* v. *Salazar.* It was decided this January 3, 2013. And basically saying that, you know, people, after *Patchak,* have the right to challenge this. And then there is a statute of limitation that is 5 or 6 years.

Ms. HANABUSA. And so, that gives them the right to challenge under the Administrative Procedures Act——

Mr. SKIBINE. That is right.

Ms. HANABUSA [continuing]. As well, correct?

Mr. SKIBINE. Yes.

Ms. HANABUSA. And have you personally experienced any challenges under the National Environmental Protection Act for decisions on the two-step process and whether or not the Assistant Secretary has really looked at all the necessary criteria under NEPA, and doing the evaluation?

Mr. SKIBINE. No, I have not personally experienced this. But, you know, I teach administrative law, and I can tell you that NEPA review in a lot of non-Indian cases is extensive, concerning what has to be taken into consideration under the environmental laws.

Ms. HANABUSA. But do you feel that these avenues have not been explored as much in the context of the two-step process?

Mr. SKIBINE. No, I think they have been. I think they have been by this administration.

Ms. HANABUSA. How about by people who believe they are aggrieved by the decision?

Mr. SKIBINE. Well, you know, basically let me put it this way. There has never been gaming on off-reservation land that was not endorsed by the local community. There has been one decision, I think in 1992, involving Siletz Tribe of Oregon, where they made a positive two-part determination and the Governor of Oregon quickly vetoed that.

Ms. HANABUSA. So, are you saying that the examples that we have seen of approvals have usually come, or have come, with the consensus of the communities, as well?

Mr. SKIBINE. Yes, except in this one case.

Ms. HANABUSA. Except in that one case.

Mr. SKIBINE. And that one case, the Governor vetoed it.

Ms. HANABUSA. And the Governor vetoed, which is his right under the two-step——

Mr. SKIBINE. That is right. Now, having said that, you know, when the local community, obviously, as we found out, may not be unified. And so that is a standard. This is why I think that if they decide to tweak the rules, I think we should keep standards for the Secretary to evaluate, instead of imposing hard and fast rules.

Ms. HANABUSA. So you are saying don't amend the statute, but maybe look at the Secretary amending his rules.

Mr. SKIBINE. Well, I think that is the proper way——

Ms. HANABUSA. Or she, amending her rules now. It is a woman.

Mr. SKIBINE. Yes, absolutely. And by the way, this was the first time that I looked at the Act as being the Udall-Young-Reagan bill. Because when it was passed, I think that Senator Inouye thought it was mostly his bill.

[Laughter.]

Ms. HANABUSA. On that note, I yield back.

Mr. YOUNG. Doctor, for your information, all the good work the House—it is sort of like the Marine Corps and the Army. We did all the work, the Marine Corps had better press corps. And we passed the Magnuson-Stevens Act, the work was done in the House, we passed this, and all the Senators take credit for it. Keep that—when you become a Senator, just keep us poor people in mind, will you?

Ms. HANABUSA. This will always be the Young bill.

Mr. YOUNG. There you go.

[Laughter.]

Mr. YOUNG. Mr. Todd, does anybody support this deal in your area?

Mr. MIELKE. We have one, within Spokane County, we have one community, a small city named Airway Heights, in which the proposed project is going to be sited, and is the only jurisdiction to re-

ceive mitigation under the agreement. They are on record as doing
it. Other than that, I would tell you that we have a former Governor, we have numerous legislators in both the House and the
Senate, we have U.S. Congresswoman, Cathy McMorris Rodgers,
two former secretaries, the current and the former Secretary of
State in the State of Washington, all in opposition, as well as the
city of Spokane, Spokane County, city of Cheney, and the list goes
on.

Mr. YOUNG. Do you have a casino in your area?

Mr. MIELKE. We do. We have, and I think this goes to the point
that many of the committee members made in the discussion with
panel one, we have another tribe known as the Coeur d'Alene
Tribe, that is about a half-hour drive, maybe a little bit more, from
the metropolitan area of Spokane. They have spent millions developing a destination resort on reservation land, and they have done
a very nice job. The Spokane Tribe that is the applicant also has
two casinos, approximately a 30- to 45-minute drive from the metropolitan area, as well.

Mr. YOUNG. So you have three casinos?

Mr. MIELKE. We have three tribal casinos on-reservation within
a 30- to 45-minute drive. And again, the Coeur d'Alene model is
one that they have reinvested every penny that they have made
back into this to make their destination resort. This application
would place an off-reservation casino near the metropolitan area.

Now, there is one more that I want to make sure that I do mention. We do have one other tribe that was granted an exemption.
And I earlier said that the Spokane Tribe has one of the largest
reservations in the Northwest. The one tribe that was granted an
exemption has one of the smallest reservations in the Northwest,
with less than 4,000 acres, 60 percent of it is below the flood plain
with no identified source of potable water to support any commercial activity. That is the one exception that was granted in our
area.

So, as we begin to take a look at this, what we are looking at
is for the tribes that have invested millions on destination resorts
on their reservation, what is the impact of a half-hour drive to a
metropolitan area with close to a half-a-million people? I think it
is significant.

Mr. YOUNG. And that goes back to the doctor, you say "tweaking." Do you have any suggestions you would like to put in writing
about tweaking? Because I am always interested in tweaking. And
I happen to agree with you in regulations. I don't agree with Dr.
Washburn. I do believe if we got together, this committee and the
Secretary, we could tweak this within 90 days. I believe that could
be done. Because you and I know how regulations work. I hate
them. Because at the 60 or 90 day comment period, they are written, nobody can really object to them, and they become law.

Now, I am going to ask you, and you don't have to answer now,
but if you have ideas that can make this thing work better, because
I happen to agree with you. I would like not to have legislation, although I will pursue legislation, because I do think there has been,
not because of Dr. Washburn, I think over the years there are people with very large sums of money that see a way of taking advantage of certain tribes. And they see how to take advantage. Three

or four get a lot of money, and nobody else gets anything. Yet they can have a detrimental effect on an existing tribal operation. That is something I think that we should be well aware of.

So, I am going to ask you to send me a tweak. Not a twitter, because I don't do that stuff, you know. Give me some ideas how you can do it.

Mr. SKIBINE. All right, thank you. Yes, I will.

Mr. YOUNG. OK, good. And Hazel, in your area, the casino they are proposing would be in Yuba County or in Colusa County?

Ms. LONGMIRE. Yuba County.

Mr. YOUNG. Oh, down below the—Marysville, in that area? Now, that interferes with the Auburn casino, does it?

Ms. LONGMIRE. Yes, it is. The territory that they are building on actually belongs to United Auburn, which is, you know, at Thunder Valley there.

Mr. YOUNG. Now, United Auburn, though, has a casino of their own, right?

Ms. LONGMIRE. Yes, they do.

Mr. YOUNG. And they don't support them building another casino, do they?

Ms. LONGMIRE. No, they don't.

Mr. YOUNG. OK. So how did they get to this Auburn land from a group from Oroville?

Ms. LONGMIRE. The Enterprise casino actually is from Oroville. Supposedly their land was sold, or it was bought way back when, when Governor Brown, Jerry Brown's father, was in office. And the Oroville Dam was being built. And that was where their land was. But there were two Enterprises, I and II.

And as in some communities, you know, there is a division of families there. So one said, "No, you are not going to live here," and the other ones, you know—but they are still all tribal members. When Enterprise II went about on their own and still had their land, you know, side-by-side with Enterprise I, and have houses there, have land into trust there, and wanted to build a casino. But they didn't want to build on their own land.

Mr. YOUNG. So they could build in Oroville?

Ms. LONGMIRE. They could if they wanted to, yes.

Mr. YOUNG. Which is about 75 miles from Colusa.

Ms. LONGMIRE. Yes.

Mr. YOUNG. Yes, OK. And about 75 miles from the Auburn casino.

Ms. LONGMIRE. Yes, sir.

Mr. YOUNG. And that would be a better location, but it isn't near the bigger market.

Ms. LONGMIRE. That is right, sir.

Mr. YOUNG. So this is all about money and—is there a tribe from Oroville? Is it a——

Ms. LONGMIRE. There are two other tribes that are up there, sir, Mooretown and Feather River—Feather Falls, rather. And there are small casinos, but they are no more than maybe a half-hour away from each other, and they work very well, you know, in balance with each other.

Mr. YOUNG. So they already have a casino.

Ms. LONGMIRE. Yes, they do.

Mr. YOUNG. OK, all right.

Ms. LONGMIRE. And they put their monies back into their business and other businesses. So——

Mr. YOUNG. OK.

Ms. LONGMIRE. You know, just as well as we have. So, you know, we put all our monies back into our education and our clinic and our dialysis and, you know, our government, our school, and our houses. That is where our money is put into.

Mr. YOUNG. OK. Madam.

Ms. HANABUSA. Hazel, I was just reading your complaint that was filed I think in December——

Ms. LONGMIRE. Yes.

Ms. HANABUSA [continuing]. Of 2012. And I just wanted to tell the professor that he is correct about the fact that your first claim for relief is actually a NEPA violation. And it seems to be that what you are saying is that what the Secretary failed to do was to consider alternatives, which is, of course, as we all know, a major criteria in looking at evaluations of——

Ms. LONGMIRE. Yes.

Ms. HANABUSA [continuing]. The EIS process. And your second claim for relief is a violation of IGRA itself.

Ms. LONGMIRE. Yes.

Ms. HANABUSA. And you are seeking in this an injunctive action. Can you tell me, subsequent to its filing, what has, I think December 14 is when you filed this case. What has happened, in terms of the procedures? I assume it is some rejudgment or, you know, something quick that is processing this?

Ms. LONGMIRE. All we have been doing since then is, well, we have been trying to meet with the Governor, with his aide, to no avail on that, well, I would say within the past 2 years we have been trying to meet.

And I think we finally met with—earlier this year—with the Governor's aide. And that was after we did our own impact study, or rather, we had Alan Meister and Clyde Barrow do an impact study for us, which the Governor asked us to do. And we did that. And——

Ms. HANABUSA. I assume, from what you are saying, that your Governor has not indicated that he will veto or he will exercise his right to say that he does not agree with this two-part——

Ms. LONGMIRE. We have not heard since this study. We have not heard from him.

Ms. HANABUSA. But you realize that if he were to take that position, this would not happen, correct? Under the two-part test.

Ms. LONGMIRE. We are hoping, yes.

Ms. HANABUSA. Thank you. Thank you, Mr. Chair.

Mr. YOUNG. I want to mention, Hazel, about the Oroville group. If my father had better foresight, I wouldn't be sitting here, because we were sheep ranchers in the area that they are claiming in Oroville was really the tailings of the mining that went on in Oroville. They offered 10,000 acres for a dollar an acre. He said, "What do I want it for? There is nothing but rock." And he was right. But little did he know they were going to build the Oroville Dam. And they took all that rock and built the dam.

Ms. LONGMIRE. That is right.

Mr. YOUNG. I would have been one rich mother. I will tell you that right now.

[Laughter.]

Ms. HANABUSA. And you wouldn't have to move to Alaska.

Mr. YOUNG. No, I would have moved to Alaska, anyway. I was going to Alaska.

I want to thank the panel. And if you have any suggestions, anything to offer to the doctor, how we can tweak this thing, I think Dr. Washburn wants to do this. He is following the law, he is under a lot of pressure. I am not happy with some of them he has issued yet, but he is doing what he has to do. And I think, if I heard him correctly, he wouldn't mind a little tweaking himself. He says it takes 2 years. It takes about 90 days, if we set our minds to it.

And if we can't do it correctly, we will do it by legislation, because I don't want this proliferation of casinos because eventually, I think the States, Madam Chair, see, I am making you chairman already, the States will say, "Why—if the Indians can do it, we can do it," and they will legalize the whole thing, and the whole thing goes down the tube. And I just don't want that to happen.

I want to thank the committee, I mean the witnesses. And I appreciate you. And we will continue working with—feel free to communicate with us. Any questions we will ask you in writing—if we have any other questions. So, God bless you and thank you.

Ms. LONGMIRE. Thank you.

Mr. YOUNG. This meeting is adjourned.

[Whereupon, at 4:45 p.m., the subcommittee was adjourned.]

[Additional Material Submitted for the Record]

PREPARED STATEMENT OF THE CALIFORNIA STATE ASSOCIATION OF COUNTIES

This testimony is submitted on behalf of the California State Association of Counties (CSAC). Founded in 1895, CSAC is the unified voice on behalf of all 58 of California's counties. The primary purpose of the association is to represent county government before the California Legislature, administrative agencies, and the Federal Government.

CSAC places a strong emphasis on educating the public about the value and need for county programs and services. Additionally, the association and its members are pleased to remain actively involved in pursuing Federal laws and regulations that provide the framework for constructive government-to-government relationships between counties and tribes.

It must be stated at the outset that CSAC reaffirms its absolute respect for the authority granted to federally recognized tribes. We also reaffirm our support for the right of Indian tribes to self-governance and recognize the need for tribes to preserve their tribal heritage and to pursue economic self-reliance.

At the same time, CSAC believes that existing Federal laws and regulations fail to address the off-reservation impacts of tribal land development, including casinos, and particularly in those instances when local land use and health and safety regulations are not being fully observed by tribes in their commercial endeavors. As we all know, commercial projects on reservation land can attract large volumes of visitors and lead to myriad impacts on the surrounding community.

The intent of this testimony is to provide a perspective from California's counties regarding the need for Congress to address what we believe are major, long-standing deficiencies in the current land-into-trust process as it relates to both gaming and non-gaming land acquisitions. In our view, the current fee-to-trust process, as authorized under the Indian Reorganization Act of 1934 (IRA) and governed by the Department of the Interior's part 151 regulations, lacks adequate standards and has led to unnecessary conflict and distrust of the Federal decisionmaking system for trust lands.

THE ROLE OF COUNTIES

There are two key reasons why the subject matter at hand is of heightened importance for California counties. First, counties are legally responsible to provide a broad scope of vital services for all members of their communities. Second, throughout the State of California and the Nation, tribal gaming has rapidly expanded, creating economic, social, environmental, health, safety, and other impacts. The facts clearly show that the mitigation and costs of such impacts increasingly fall upon county government.

Every Californian, including all tribal members, depend upon county government for a broad range of critical services, from public safety and transportation, to waste management and disaster relief. California counties are responsible for nearly 700 programs, including, but not limited to, the following: local law enforcement, public health, fire protection, family support, probation, jails, child and adult protective services, roads and bridges, and flood control. Notably, most of these services are provided to residents both outside and inside of city limits.

Unlike the exercise of land use control, programs such as public health, welfare, and jail services are provided—and often mandated—regardless of whether a recipient resides within a city or in the unincorporated area of the county. These vital public services are delivered to California residents through their 58 counties. It is no exaggeration to say that county government is essential to the quality of life for over 37 million Californians. In addition, because county governments have very little authority to independently raise taxes and increase revenues, the ability to adequately mitigate tribal commercial endeavors is critical, or all county services could be put at risk.

Counties have a legal responsibility to properly provide for and protect the health, safety, and general welfare of the members of their communities. However, California counties' efforts in this regard have been significantly impacted by the rapid expansion of Indian gaming. Although certain tribes and counties have reached local agreements for the mitigation of off-reservation impacts on services that counties are required to provide, many others have not. In the absence of local agreements, counties must bear the full cost and burden of addressing the off-reservation impacts associated with commercial gaming enterprises.

Because of counties' integral role in the daily lives of it citizens, and in consideration of the impacts to communities created by ever-expanding tribal business ventures, counties should be viewed as indispensible to any discussion involving the Bureau of Indian Affairs' (BIA) land-into-trust process. To follow is a description of what CSAC regards as the long-standing defects in the trust acquisition process, as well as a series of recommendations for how the process should be fixed.

THE DEFICIENCIES OF THE CURRENT LAND-INTO-TRUST PROCESS

The fundamental problem with the trust acquisition process is that Congress has not set standards under which any delegated trust land authority would be applied by BIA. The relevant section of Federal law, section 5 of the IRA, reads as follows. "The Secretary of the Interior is hereby authorized in his discretion, to acquire [by various means] any interest in lands, water rights, or surface rights to lands, within or without reservations . . . for the purpose of providing land to Indians." 25 U.S.C. § 465.

The aforementioned general and undefined congressional guidance, as implemented by the Department of the Interior in its part 151 regulations, has resulted in a trust land process that fails to meaningfully include legitimate interests, provide adequate transparency to the public, or demonstrate fundamental balance in trust land decisions. The unsatisfactory process has created significant controversy, serious conflicts between tribes and States, counties and local governments—including litigation costly to all parties—and broad distrust of the fairness of the system.

One of CSAC's central concerns with the current trust acquisition process is the severely limited role that state and local governments play. The implications of losing jurisdiction over local lands are very significant, including the loss of tax base, loss of planning and zoning authority, and the loss of environmental and other regulatory power. Yet, State, county and local governments are afforded limited, and often late, notice of a pending trust land application, and, under the current regulations, are asked to provide comments on two narrow issues only: (1) potential jurisdictional conflicts; and, (2) loss of tax revenues.

Moreover, the notice that local governments receive typically does not include the actual fee-to-trust application and often does not indicate how the applicant tribe intends to use the land. Further, in some cases, tribes have proposed a trust acquisition without identifying a use for the land; in other cases, tribes have identified a non-intensive, mundane use, only to change the use to heavy economic development, such as gaming or energy projects, soon after the land is acquired in trust.

Local governments also are often forced to resort to Freedom of Information Act (FOIA) requests to ascertain if a petition for an Indian lands determination—a key step in the process for a parcel of land to qualify for gaming—has been filed in their jurisdiction. Because many tribal land acquisitions ultimately will be used for economic development purposes—including gaming activities—there are often significant unmitigated impacts to the surrounding community, including environmental and economic impacts. Unfortunately, current law does not provide any incentive for tribes and affected local governments to enter into agreements for the mitigation of off-reservation impacts.

While the Department of the Interior understands the increased impacts and conflicts inherent in recent trust land decisions, it has not crafted regulations that strike a reasonable balance between tribes seeking new trust lands and the States and local governments experiencing unacceptable impacts. Indeed, the current notification process embodied in the part 151 regulations is, in practice, insufficient and falls far short of providing local governments with the level of detail needed to adequately respond to proposed trust land acquisitions. Accordingly, a legislative effort is needed to meet the fundamental interests of both tribes and local governments.

CARCIERI V. SALAZAR—A HISTORIC OPPORTUNITY

On February 24, 2009, the U.S. Supreme Court issued its landmark decision on Indian trust lands in *Carcieri* v. *Salazar*. The Court held that the Secretary of the Interior lacks authority to take land into trust on behalf of Indian tribes that were not under the jurisdiction of the Federal Government upon enactment of the IRA in 1934.

Because the *Carcieri* decision has definitively confirmed the Secretary's lack of authority to take land into trust for post-1934 tribes, Congress has the opportunity not just to address the issue of the Secretary's authority under the current failed fee-to-trust system, but to reassert its primary authority for these decisions by setting specific standards for taking land into trust that address the main shortcomings of the trust land process.

In the wake of this significant court decision, varied proposals for reversing the *Carcieri* decision have been generated, some proposing administrative action and others favoring a congressional approach. Today's hearing, like several hearings before it, is a recognition of the significance of the *Carcieri* decision and the need to consider legislative action.

We believe that the responsibility to address the implications of *Carcieri* clearly rests with Congress and that a decision to do so in isolation of the larger problems of the fee-to-trust system would represent an historic missed opportunity. Indeed, a legislative resolution that hastily returns the trust land system to its status before *Carcieri* will be regarded as unsatisfactory to counties, local governments, and the people we serve. Rather than a "fix," such a result would only perpetuate a broken system, where the non-tribal entities most affected by the trust acquisition process are without a meaningful role. Ultimately, this would undermine the respectful government-to-government relationship that is necessary for both tribes and neighboring governments to fully develop, thrive, and serve the people dependent upon them for their well being.

Our primary recommendation to the subcommittee and to Congress is this: Do not advance a congressional response to *Carcieri* that allows the Secretary of the Interior to return to the flawed fee-to-trust process. Rather, carefully examine, with input from tribal, State and local governments, what reforms are necessary to "fix" the fee-to-trust process and refine the definition of Indian lands under the Indian Gaming Regulatory Act (IGRA). Concurrently, the Secretary of the Interior should determine the impacts of the *Carcieri* decision, including the specific tribes affected and the nature and urgency of their need, so that a more focused and effective legislative remedy can be undertaken.

The *Carcieri* decision presents Congress with an opportunity to carefully exercise its constitutional authority for fee-to-trust acquisitions and to define the respective roles of Congress and the executive branch in trust land decisions. Additionally, it affords Congress with the opportunity to establish clear and specific congressional standards and processes to guide trust land decisions in the future. A clear definition of roles is acutely needed regardless of whether trust and recognition decisions are ultimately made by Congress, as provided in the Constitution, or the executive branch under a congressional grant of authority.

It should be noted that Congress has the power to not provide new standard-less authority to the executive branch for trust land decisions and instead retain its own authority to make these decisions on a case-by-case basis as it has done in the past, although decreasingly in recent years. Whether or not Congress chooses to retain its authority or to delegate it in some way, it owes it to tribes and to States, counties, local governments and communities, to provide clear direction to the Secretary of the Interior to make trust land decisions according to specific congressional standards and to eliminate much of the conflict inherent in such decisions under present practice.

Looking ahead, we respectfully urge members of this subcommittee to consider both sides of the problem in any legislation seeking to address the trust land process post-*Carcieri*, namely: (1) the absence of authority to acquire trust lands, which affects post-1934 tribes, and (2) the lack of meaningful standards and a fair and open process, which affects States, local governments, businesses and non-tribal communities. As Congress considers the trust land issue, it should undertake reform that is in the interests of all affected parties.

Some of the more important new standards should be as follows:

Notice and Transparency

(1) **Require Full Disclosure from the Tribes on Trust Land Applications and Other Indian Land Decisions, and Fair Notice and Transparency from the BIA.** The part 151 regulations are not specific and do not require sufficient information about tribal plans to use the land proposed for trust status. As a result, it is very difficult for affected parties (local and State governments, and the public) to determine the nature of the tribal proposal, evaluate the impacts, and provide meaningful comments.

BIA should be directed to require tribes to provide reasonably detailed information to State and affected local governments, as well as the public, about the proposed uses of the land early on, not unlike the public information required for planning, zoning and permitting on the local level. This assumes even greater importance since local planning, zoning and permitting are being preempted by the trust land decision; accordingly, information about intended uses is reasonable and fair to require.

Legislative and regulatory changes need to be made to ensure that affected governments receive timely notice of fee-to-trust applications and petitions for Indian land determinations in their jurisdiction and have adequate time to provide meaningful input. Indian lands determinations, a critical step for a tribe to take land into trust for gaming purposes, is conducted in secret without notice to affected counties or any real opportunity for input. As previously indicated, counties are often forced to file a FOIA request to even determine if an application was filed and the basis for the petition.

Notice for trust and other land actions for tribes that go to counties and other governments is not only very limited in coverage, the opportunity to comment is minimal; this must change. A new paradigm is needed where counties are considered meaningful and constructive stakeholders in Indian land-related determinations. For too long, counties have been excluded from providing input in critical Department of Interior decisions and policy formation that directly affects their communities. This remains true today as evidenced by new policies being announced by the administration without input from local government organizations.

The corollary is that consultation with counties and local governments must be substantive, include all affected communities, and provide an opportunity for public comment. Under part 151, BIA does not invite comment by third parties even though they may experience major negative impacts, although it will accept and review such comments. BIA accepts comments only from the affected State and the local government with legal jurisdiction over the land and, from those parties, only on the narrow question of tax revenue loss, government services currently provided to the subject parcels, and zoning conflicts. As a result, under current BIA practice, trust acquisition requests are reviewed under a very one-sided and incomplete record that does not provide real consultation or an adequate representation of the consequences of the decision. Broad notice of trust applications should be required with at least 90 days to respond.

(2) **The BIA Should Define "Tribal Need" and Require Specific Information about Need from the Tribes.** The BIA regulations provide inadequate guidance as to what constitutes legitimate tribal need for a trust land acquisition. There are no standards other than the stipulation that the land is necessary to facilitate tribal self-determination, economic development or Indian housing. These standards can be met by virtually any trust land request, regardless of how successful the tribe is or how much land it already owns. As a result, there are numerous examples of BIA taking additional land into trust for economically and governmentally self-sufficient tribes already having wealth and large land bases.

Congress should consider developing standards requiring justification of the need and purpose for acquisition of additional trust lands so that the acquisition process does not continue to be a "blank check" for removing land from State and local jurisdiction/ Notably, CSAC supports a lower threshold for acquisition of trust land that will be used only for non-gaming or non-intensive economic purposes, including governmental uses and housing projects.

(3) Applications Should Require Specific Representations of Intended Uses. Changes in use should not be permitted without further reviews, including environmental impacts, and application of relevant procedures and limitations. Such further review should have the same notice, comment, and consultation as the initial application. The law also should be changed to explicitly authorize restrictions and conditions to be placed on land going into trust that further the interests of both affected tribes and other affected governments.

(4) Tribes that Reach Local Intergovernmental Agreements to Address Jurisdiction and Environmental Impacts Should Have a Streamlined Process. The legal framework should encourage tribes to reach intergovernmental agreements to address off-reservation project impacts by reducing the threshold for demonstrating need when such agreements are in place. Tribes, States, and counties need a process that is less costly and more efficient. The virtually unfettered discretion contained in the current process, due to the lack of clear standards, almost inevitably creates conflict and burdens the system. A process that encourages cooperation and communication provides a basis to expedite decisions and reduce costs and frustration for all involved.

It should be noted that an approach that encourages intergovernmental agreements between a tribe and local government affected by fee-to-trust applications is required and working well under recent California State gaming compacts. Not only does such an approach offer the opportunity to streamline the application process, it can also help to ensure the success of the tribal project within the local community. The establishment of a trust land system that incentivizes intergovernmental agreements between tribes and local governments is at the heart of CSAC's fee-to-trust reform recommendations and should be a top priority for Congress.

(5) Establish Clear Objective Standards for Agency Exercise of Discretion in Making Fee-to-Trust Decisions. The lack of meaningful standards or any objective criteria in fee-to-trust decisions made by the BIA have been long criticized by the U.S. Government Accountability Office and local governments. For example, BIA requests only minimal information about the impacts of such acquisitions on local communities and trust land decisions are not governed by a requirement to balance the benefit to the tribe against the impact to the local community. As a result, there are well-known and significant impacts of trust land decisions on communities and States, with consequent controversy and delay and distrust of the process.

Furthermore, the BIA has the specific mission to serve Indians and tribes and is granted broad discretion to decide in favor of tribes. In order to reasonably balance the interests of tribes and local governments, the executive branch should be given clear direction from Congress regarding considerations of need and mitigation of impacts to approve a trust land acquisition. However any delegation of authority is resolved, Congress must specifically direct clear and balanced standards that ensure that trust land requests cannot be approved where the negative impacts to other parties outweigh the benefit to the tribe.

The attached fee-to-trust legislative reform proposal developed by CSAC seeks to address the inequities and flaws in the current trust land system. The centerpiece of the reform package is a proposal that would provide an incentive for tribes and local governments to enter into judicially enforceable mitigation agreements. Additionally, the proposal would remedy the aforementioned defects in the fee-to-trust process related to inadequate notification and consultation requirements, as well as address other significant shortcomings in the trust land system.

PENDING LEGISLATION

As stated above, congressional action must address the critical repairs needed in the fee-to-trust process. Unfortunately, legislation currently pending in the House (H.R. 279 and H.R. 666) fails to set clear standards for taking land into trust, to properly balance the roles and interests of tribes, State, local and Federal Governments in these decisions, and to clearly address the apparent usurpation of authority by the executive branch over Congress' constitutional authority over tribal recognition.

H.R. 279, in particular, serves to expand the undelegated power of the Department of the Interior by expanding the definition of an Indian tribe under the IRA to any community the Secretary "acknowledges to exist as an Indian Tribe [empha-

61

sis added].'' In doing so, the effect of the bill is to facilitate off-reservation activities by tribes and perpetuate the inconsistent standards that have been used to create tribal entities. Such a "solution" causes controversy and conflict rather than an open process which, particularly in States such as California, is needed to address the varied circumstances of local governments and tribes.

IGRA

While the IRA provides the Secretary of the Interior with the authority to take land into trust for the benefit of Indian tribes, IGRA provides the framework for tribes to conduct gaming on trust land. Under IGRA, casino-style gaming is authorized on lands located within or contiguous to the boundaries of a tribe's reservation as it existed on October 17, 1988 (the date of IGRA's enactment). Although the act prohibits gaming on land taken into trust or restricted status for a tribe after the aforementioned date, Congress authorized several notable exceptions to the prohibition. Pursuant to section 20 of IGRA, gaming is allowed under the following circumstances:

- The land is part of the initial reservation of an Indian tribe acknowledged by the Secretary under the Federal acknowledgment process;
- The restoration of land for a tribe that is restored to Federal recognition;
- If, after consultation with the Indian tribe, other nearby tribes, and appropriate State and local officials, the Secretary determines that a gaming establishment on newly acquired lands would be in the best interest of the Indian tribe and its members and would not be detrimental to the surrounding community and the Governor concurs in the Secretary's determination;
- The land is taken into trust for a tribe as part of a land claim settlement.

The passage of IGRA has substantially increased both tribal and non-tribal investor interest in having lands acquired in trust so that economic development projects, otherwise prohibited under State law, could be built. The opportunities under IGRA were also a factor in causing many tribal groups that were not recognized as tribes in 1934 to seek Federal recognition and trust land in the past 20 years.

Further, tribes have more aggressively sought lands that are of substantially greater value to State and local governments, even when distant from the tribe's existing reservation, because such locations are far more marketable for various economic purposes. The result has been increasing conflict between tribes and State and local governments.

In California in 2011, 2012 and 2013 alone, there were approximately 40 applications from tribes to take land into trust consisting of approximately 9,450 acres of land. California's unique cultural history and geography, and the fact that there are over 100 federally recognized tribes in the State, contributes to the fact that no two land-into-trust applications are alike.

It should be noted that some tribes are seeking to have land located far from their aboriginal location deemed "restored land" under IGRA; if successful—and if Congress were to restore the Secretary's trust land acquisition authority for post-1934 tribes—this would allow the land to be eligible for gaming even without the support of the Governor or local communities, as would be otherwise required. Restored tribes are an exception for gaming that circumvents the intended two-part determination process that empowers a state to manage the location and growth of gaming.

CSAC's policy with respect to gaming on restored lands is one that reflects the importance of local government and individual tribal government relationships and the uniqueness of each local situation. Indeed, there are a number of examples of California counties working cooperatively with tribes on a government-to-government basis on issues of common concern to both parties, not just gaming-related issues. Based on this cooperation, tribes and counties have forged mutually beneficial agreements that address the impacts of tribal development projects.

At the same time, there are examples of tribal governments that have not complied with the requirements of IGRA or California's Tribal-State Gaming Compacts. In these instances, conflict has ensued and the county has been left to address the impacts associated with the tribe's development.

As provided for in CSAC's fee-to-trust reform proposal, the overriding principle supported by the association is that when tribes are permitted to engage in gaming activities under Federal legislation, judicially enforceable agreements between counties and tribal governments must be required. Such agreements should fully mitigate local impacts from a tribal government's business activities and fully identify the governmental services to be provided by the county to that tribe.

POTENTIAL CHANGES TO THE FEDERAL ACKNOWLEDGMENT PROCESS

Earlier this year, the Department of the Interior released a discussion draft of potential changes to the Department's part 83 process for acknowledging certain Indian groups as federally recognized tribes. The intent of the proposed draft is for BIA to solicit comments identifying potential changes to the Federal acknowledgment process to improve the integrity of the Bureau's decisions to recognize particular groups as Indian tribes.

The Federal acknowledgment process is the Department's regulatory procedure by which petitioning groups that meet the regulatory criteria are "acknowledged" as federally recognized Indian tribes with a government-to-government relationship with the United States. Once an Indian tribe receives formal recognition, the tribe and its members are eligible for certain benefits, as well as subject to certain protections. It also means that the tribe may be eligible to conduct gaming operations under IGRA.

CSAC is interested in the topic of Federal acknowledgment because there are potentially hundreds of Indian groups in California that may desire recognition from the Federal Government and which may desire to have land removed from State and local jurisdiction through the fee-to-trust process, particularly for gaming purposes, upon or in connection with acknowledgment. The association takes great interest in any decisionmaking process that may lead to the removal of land from State and local jurisdiction, for reasons previously discussed in this testimony.

CSAC understands that the current acknowledgment process has been criticized as expensive, burdensome, opaque, and inflexible. We believe, however, that modifications to the current process, if any, to address these criticisms, must not compromise the integrity of BIA's decisions to recognize a group as an Indian tribe—a political entity with a distinct "government-to-government relationship with the United States" and that has been in continuous existence as a political entity and social community since the time of first contact with non-Indians.

Acknowledgement confers significant political and economic benefits to the recognized tribe and creates a powerful government-to-government relationship stretching into perpetuity. Because counties interact with federally recognized tribes on important matters ranging from child welfare to economic development to prevention of environmental and cultural degradation, CSAC is particularly interested in the accuracy of acknowledgement decisions. Moreover, county governments often already have a relationship with an unrecognized tribe or group, and can contribute directly to the Bureau's investigation.

We believe that the acknowledgment process would be greatly improved if the Bureau were required to affirmatively seek input from local governments concerning petitions for acknowledgments at the earliest opportunity. Moreover, CSAC believes that acknowledgment must be objective, based on verifiable evidence received from all interested parties, and made according to uniformly applied and rigorous criteria. In short, such an important decision should be made with deliberate care.

Unfortunately, the Department's proposed draft changes would diminish the rights of local governments to participate in the acknowledgment process. First, while the current part 83 regulations provide for limited and constructive participation of Informed and Interested Parties, the draft would eliminate the opportunity of such parties, including local governments, to appeal a final acknowledgment determination. The ability to file an administrative appeal with the Interior Board of Indian Appeals provides a check on improper decisions by BIA and should be maintained as part of the process.

Additionally, CSAC has significant concerns with the following proposed changes: the unfair page limit on interested party submissions; the one-way requirement that interested parties must submit their evidence and argument to petitioners, but not vice versa; the ability for petitioners to cease active review whenever they want, despite the cost and disruption caused to interested parties; the elimination of the requirement for an interested party to file a notice of intent, which serves as early notice to local governments; the denial of technical assistance to interested parties, even though it is provided to petitioners; and, providing petitioners, but not interested parties, the right to submit evidence at a hearing. The aforementioned changes are all one-sided in favor of petitioners, and they go too far.

Because of the impact that IGRA has had on acknowledgement, restoration and reaffirmation, CSAC recommends that, in addition to removing the problematic proposals discussed above, BIA should include the following steps in the "conversation of the draft discussion."

- Solicit input from and convene consultation meetings with local governments, including counties in particular, concerning acknowledgment petitions at the earliest opportunity. Counties have government-to-government relationships with tribes affecting a variety of important interests from child welfare, to gaming, to environmental protection and mitigation of off-reservation impacts created by on-reservation development, including gaming in particular. As a result, counties are uniquely positioned to contribute important evidence to the acknowledgment process. Additionally, counties should be consulted prior to the Bureau authorizing re-petition by a previously denied petitioner.

- Facilitate and encourage constructive public participation in the review process. Several consultation hearings should be scheduled in California where there are more tribes than any other State petitioning for Federal recognition or seeking reaffirmation.
- Additionally, since newly acknowledged tribes are a clear and indisputable exception under section 20 of IGRA, although a separate process, a stringent and transparent fee-to-trust process with significant input from all stakeholders must be considered regarding "initial" reservation lands. Of course, BIA acquired trust land is not currently available to newly acknowledged tribes as a result of the *Carcieri* decision, and this fact should be acknowledged by BIA.

In sum, California counties are uniquely interested in the acknowledgement process not only because of the sheer number of current and potential petitions, but also due to the potential for tribal recognition to lead to the removal of land from State and local jurisdiction. Additionally, due to their government-to-government relations with tribes that span a host of matters important to all levels of government, California counties have significant interest in which groups are granted Federal recognition status. Finally, California counties have important information to contribute to the acknowledgement process that should be considered when acknowledgement decisions are made. Accordingly, the Bureau should be required to fully engage and solicit information from counties concerning acknowledgement petitions, or authorization for re-petitions.

CONCLUSION

We ask members of the subcommittee and Congress as a whole to thoughtfully consider the recommendations that we have submitted as part of this testimony. In particular, as the subcommittee considers options for addressing the implications of *Carcieri,* we urge you to incorporate the aforementioned fee-to-trust reforms as part of any legislative proposal that may emerge. Indeed, Congress must take the lead in any legal repair for inequities caused by the Supreme Court's action, but absolutely should not do so without addressing these critically important and long-overdue reforms.

CSAC's proposals are common-sense modifications that, if enacted, will eliminate some of the most controversial and problematic elements of the current trust land acquisition process. The result would help States, local governments, and non-tribal stakeholders. These reforms also would assist trust land applicants by guiding their requests toward a collaborative process and, in doing so, reduce the delay and controversy that now routinely accompany acquisition requests.

We also urge Members to reject any "one-size-fits-all" solution to these issues. In our view, IGRA itself has often represented such an approach, and as a result has caused many problems throughout the Nation where the sheer number of tribal entities and the great disparity among them requires a thoughtful case-by-case analysis of each tribal land acquisition decision.

Thank you for considering these views.

COMPREHENSIVE FEE-TO-TRUST REFORM PROPOSAL

Section 5 of the Indian Reorganization Act, 25 U.S.C. § 465

The Secretary of the Interior is authorized, in his discretion, to acquire, through purchase, relinquishment, gift, exchange, or assignment, any interest in lands, water rights, or surface rights to lands, within or without existing reservations, including trust or otherwise restricted allotments, whether the allottee be living or deceased, for the purpose of providing land for Indians.

For the acquisition of such lands, interests in lands, water rights, and surface rights, and for expenses incident to such acquisition, there is authorized to be appropriated, out of any funds in the Treasury not otherwise appropriated, a sum not to exceed $2,000,000 in any one fiscal year: Provided, that no part of such funds shall be used to acquire additional land outside of the exterior boundaries of Navajo Indian Reservation for the Navajo Indians in Arizona, nor in New Mexico, in the event that legislation to define the exterior boundaries of the Navajo Indian Reservation in New Mexico, and for other purposes, or similar legislation, becomes law.

The unexpended balances of any appropriations made pursuant to this section shall remain available until expended.

Title to any lands or rights acquired pursuant to this act or the act of July 28, 1955 (69 Stat. 392), as amended (25 U.S.C. 608 et seq.) shall be taken in the name of the United States in trust for the Indian tribe or individual Indian for which the land is acquired, and such lands or rights shall be exempt from State and local taxation.

The Secretary may acquire land in trust pursuant to this section where the applicant has identified a specific use of the land and:

(a)   the Indian tribe or individual Indian applicant has executed enforceable agreements with each jurisdictional local government addressing the impacts of the proposed trust acquisition; or

(b)   in the absence of the agreements identified in subsection (a):

(1)   the Indian tribe or individual Indian demonstrates, and the Secretary determines, that:

(A)   the land will be used for non-economic purposes, including for religious, cultural, tribal housing, or governmental facilities, and the applicant lacks sufficient trust land for that purpose; or

(B)   the land will be used for economic or gaming purposes and the applicant has not achieved economic self-sufficiency and lacks sufficient trust land for that purpose;

and

(2)   the Secretary determines, after consulting with appropriate State and local officials, that the acquisition would not be detrimental to the surrounding community and that all significant jurisdictional conflicts and impacts, including increased costs of services, lost revenues, and environmental impacts, have been mitigated to the extent practicable.

(c)   notice and a copy of any application, partial or complete, to have land acquired in trust shall be provided by the Secretary to the State and affected local government units within twenty (20) days of receipt of the application, or of any supplement to it. The Secretary shall provide affected local governmental units at least ninety (90) days to submit comments from receipt of notice and a copy of the complete application to have land acquired in trust.

(d)   a material change in use of existing tribal trust land that significantly increases impacts, including gaming or gaming-related uses, shall require approval of the Secretary under this section, and satisfy the requirements of the National Environmental Policy Act, 42 U.S.C. § 4321 et seq., and, if applicable, the Indian Gaming Regulatory Act, 25 U.S.C. § 2701 et seq.;

(1)   the Secretary shall notify the State and affected local government units within twenty (20) days of any change in use in trust land initiated by an applicant under this subsection.

(2)   as soon as practicable following any change in use in trust land initiated prior to review and approval under this section, the Secretary shall take steps to stop the new use, including suit in Federal court, upon application by an affected local government;

(3)   any person may file an action under 5 U.S.C. § 701 et seq. to compel the Secretary to enjoin any change in use in trust land initiated prior to review and approval under this section.

(e)   notwithstanding any other provisions of law, the Secretary is authorized to include restrictions on use in the deed transferred to the United States to hold land in trust for the benefit of the Indian tribe or individual Indian and shall consider restricting use in cases involving significant jurisdictional and land use conflicts upon application of governments having jurisdiction over the land;

(f)   any agreement executed pursuant to subsection (a) of this section shall be deemed approved by the Secretary and enforceable according to the terms of the agreement upon acquisition in trust of land by the Secretary;

(g)   the Secretary shall promulgate regulations implementing these amendments within 365 days of enactment.

PREPARED STATEMENT OF THE CONFEDERATED SALISH AND KOOTENAI TRIBES
(CSKT), FLATHEAD INDIAN RESERVATION, MONTANA

INTRODUCTION

On Wednesday, May 29, 2013, the Department of the Interior (DOI) published a notice in the Federal Register proposing a rule to revise section 151.12 of the regulations codified at 25 CFR part 151, which govern the acquisition of land in trust for tribes and individual Indians. The proposed rule is intended to address changes in the applicability of the Quiet Title Act (QTA) as interpreted by the Supreme Court in *Match-E-Be-Nash She-Wish Band of Potawatomi Indians v. Patchak,* 132 S. Ct. 2199 (2012).

The CSKT support the DOI's efforts to promulgate regulations which begin to address the uncertainty and damaging impacts created by the *Patchak* decision. The CSKT believe the rules should be further revised and strengthened

We thank the DOI for its continued work on behalf of Indian tribes and for the opportunity to comment. We strongly encourage continued revision of the fee-to-trust regulations for the benefit of all Indian Nations following the completion of this rulemaking process. We urge bold regulatory changes and streamlining of the fee-to-trust process for (1) on-reservation acquisitions and (2) off-reservation acquisitions. We also urge an examination of the contributing factors that have resulted in a fee-to-trust backlog in front of the Interior Board of Indian Appeals (IBIA).

BACKGROUND

The Department's regulations at 25 CFR part 151 implement the Secretary's authority to acquire land in trust for tribes and individual Indians found in 25 U.S.C. § 465 (the Indian Reorganization Act), as well as in other land acquisition statutes.

In 1996, the Department revised its part 151 regulations to include section 151.12(b), which created a 30-day waiting period following publication in the Federal Register or newspaper of general circulation of a final agency trust acquisition determination, before the Department would actually acquire trust title to the land. The 30-day waiting period was added in response to court rulings holding that the Quiet Title Act (QTA) barred judicial review of the Department's trust acquisition decisions once title was acquired by the Secretary.

On June 18, 2012, the Supreme Court issued its decision in *Match-E-Be-Nash-She-Wish Band of Potawatomi Indians v. Patchak,* 132 S.Ct. 2199 (2012).

The *Patchak* decision holds that the QTA *does not* bar challenges to trust acquisition decisions under the Administrative Procedure Act (APA) after the United States has acquired trust title to the property, unless the plaintiff asserts an ownership interest in the property. Given this change in the law, the 30-day waiting period in section 151.12(b) is no longer necessary, since persons wishing to challenge trust acquisitions may do so at any time within a 6-year statute of limitations provided in the APA.

The Department's proposed rule removes the 30-day waiting period and revises section 151.12 to clarify the Departmental process for trust acquisitions, is primarily based on whether the decision is issued by the Assistant Secretary—Indian Affairs (AS–IA) (*a final agency determination*) or by a Bureau of Indian Affairs (BIA) official **in which case the decision is not a final agency action and is subject to administrative appeal.**

The rule also provides additional notice requirements for decisions issued by BIA officials, in an effort to ensure that all interested parties, known and unknown, are notified of the decision and their administrative appeal rights.

CSKT Comments on the Proposed Regulations

The *Patchak* decision changed the law applicable to land acquired in trust for Tribes and individual Indians. In response, the Department's proposed rule published on May 29, 2013, was to clarify when a 30-day waiting period was applicable, rather than to clarify and redefine what a mandatory trust acquisition is and what decisions are subject to appeal.

In our opinion, the BIA should be developing regulations that make **all on-reservation fee- to-trust decisions a mandatory trust acquisition.**

In addition to making the 30-day waiting period in section 151.12(b) unnecessary, the *Patchak* decision introduced a huge amount of uncertainty into the fee-to-trust process, subjecting tribes and individual Indians to the threat of potential litigation for 6 years from the time of the trust acquisition.

The uncertainty created by the *Patchak* decision is causing uncertainty for tribes' ability to develop land that they have acquired in trust. How can you obtain financing for a project on newly converted trust property if a potential appeal on the trust action can occur 6 years down the road? If local lenders were aware of this potential occurrence, tribes and individuals would likely never receive mortgage or financing assistance on newly converted trust property.

For the CSKT, each acquired fee parcel put in trust costs the tribal government an average of $5,000 per parcel of (non-Federal) tribal dollars. Since 2009, the CSKT have put an estimated 174 parcels into Trust status. Fee to trust actions have been tracked and reported annually by the DOI since 2009. Twenty seven States are engaged in fee-to-trust work, and the CSKT lead the Nation in the number of fee-to-trust transactions completed.

For the CSKT, 172 approved fee-to-trust actions have been on-reservation acquisitions. Two fee-to-trust acquisitions have been "off-reservation" trust acquisitions, for a total of 174 fee to trust acquisitions.

In addition to the 174 approved acquisitions, since 2009, the CSKT have worked to afford protection to longstanding historic religious and cultural sites of great importance to the Salish and Kootenai people (the Medicine Tree and Kootenai Falls sites). Those two off reservation applications have been appealed to the IBIA in the last 120 days.

Ninety-eight percent of all fee-to-trust decisions are made at the local level and the majority of all fee-to-trust acquisitions *are not for gaming purposes.* Ninety nine percent of all fee-to-trust actions are non-gaming related according to a DOI fee-to-trust report issued on August 29, 2013. However the controversy surrounding off-reservation acquisitions for gaming so dominates this issue that rulemaking in this area is such that the tail is clearly wagging the dog.

Most fee-to-trust acquisitions are for agricultural, infrastructure, housing and economic development reasons. Therefore, while clarifying notice provisions, the DOI should modify the proposed regulatory change further and clarify that on-reservation fee-to-trust decisions will be treated as mandatory trust acquisitions (effective upon decision).

Gaming-related fee-to-trust acquisitions take longer than any other acquisitions, typically require extensive NEPA compliance, and in many cases are subject to political review as the Governor of the State must concur with the decision. This process theoretically subjects tribes' economic efforts to the review and concurrence by a State official even when the proposed gaming facility is in the middle of the reservation on land that in all likelihood was illegally converted from trust-to-fee to start with.

It is time for the DOI to take a firm stand in support of tribes' authority to put land into trust **within the reservation boundaries.**

The best way to address the problems created by the *Patchak* decision would be for Congress to pass *Patchak-fix* legislation. For this reason, in addition to promulgating this limited administrative fix, the Department must continue to push for and strongly support a legislative fix to address the majority of the problems created by the *Patchak* decision.

With respect to trust acquisition decisions made by BIA officials (*e.g.,* Regional Directors, Superintendents, or the BIA Director), which are not final for the Department, the proposed rule makes clear that the requirement for exhaustion of administrative remedies is applicable **only to these decisions.** Why not treat all on-reservation fee-to-trust acquisitions as mandatory trust acquisitions?

The CSKT maintain that the DOI should recommend regulatory changes that make sense and which are cost effective. Why subject the *majority of BIA fee-to-trust decisions to an exhaustive, expensive administrative review and possible appeal? This does not make sense for various reasons including the stated goal of the DOI to reduce the backlog of fee to trust land applications.*

In addition, the proposed rule adds a requirement that the BIA must provide actual notice (by mail or personal delivery) of the BIA official's decision to take the land in trust and the right to file an administrative appeal under 25 CFR part 2 to all known interested parties (parties who have made themselves known, in writing, to the deciding official) and to State and local governments with jurisdiction over the land. Proposed section 151.12(d)(2)(ii).

The CSKT believe that any appeal filed must include (1) a mandatory appeal bond; and (2) the appellant must be a person whose own direct economic interest is adversely affected by the action and or decision. It is time for the BIA and IBIA to support an expedited process that eliminates frivolous appeals.

The CSKT urge the Department to place a time limit on the IBIA review. For example, if after 150 days the IBIA fails to make a decision, then the Assistant Secretary will take the recommendation of the Regional BIA Director and make the decision final. Some tribes have waited years for an IBIA review and decision. These indefinite appeals cost time and money and prevent the tribes from exercising authority over tribal-owned land.

While a process already exists in 25 CFR part 2 that allows the Assistant Secretary to pull an appeal from the IBIA and issue a decision that is final for the Department, see 25 CFR § 2.20, there are some significant limitations to this process.

Revise this portion of the regulations to mandate that the Assistant Secretary takes jurisdiction over the matter, and makes a decision. If the Assistant Secretary issues the decision, it is final for the Department. Perhaps all non-gaming fee-to-trust decisions should be exempt from IBIA review.

The Department should consider generally revising the regulations to bring them up to date, because many of the provisions are outdated. We urge the Department to revise outdated regulations so that it can more efficiently and effectively handle all pending fee-to-trust applications and thereby reduce the existing backlog.

A summary of our recommendations in table form is as follows:

	25 CFR Section 151.10	25 CFR Section 151.11	25 CFR Section 151.12	IBIA Issues
Description:	On-reservation fee-to-trust acquisitions.	Off-reservation fee-to-trust acquisitions.	Clarifies Dept. process and a 30 day waiting period.	
CSKT Recommend:	Redefine and treat all on-reservation acquisitions as mandatory acquisitions with no appeal.	Should be treated as discretionary acquisitions but expand definitions to include acquisitions for cultural and historic reasons that are within the Tribes aboriginal area. *Concentrate on Tribal reasons and benefits rather than perceived State and local government impact.*	The Tribes believe that any appeal filed must include (1) a mandatory appeal bond and the (2) appellant must be a person whose own direct economic interest is adversely affected by the action and/or decision.	Place a time limit on IBIA review and decision—i.e. 150 days. Adequately fund and staff the office. Establish a goal to eliminate the backlog of pending fee-to-trust decisions.

In summary, much work remains to be done on the DOI BIA regulations governing fee-to-trust acquisitions. The process should place the concerns of the Indian community at a higher level than the concerns of the non-Indian public. Look at our situation as but one example. Our aboriginal lands constituted over 20 million acres of western Montana. When we signed our Treaty in 1855 we reserved just over 1.3 million acres for our exclusive use. Less than 50 years later the Allotment Acts were passed and so much land was taken from us—in direct violation of the language of our Treaty—that we became the minority land holder on our own Reservation. By purchasing back reservation lands whenever they came up for sale over the course of the last half-century a majority of the lands on our Reservation are in now in trust. The DOI should facilitate this process, not make it overly burdensome. Please revise the regulations to distinguish between on and off-reservation trust acquisitions.

Every Federal process has a timeframe for action. Bring the IBIA to the reality of today, impose deadlines and adequately fund and staff the function. Tribes should not have to wait for years for decisions regarding property they purchase and own—trust landowners deserve better.

We urge you to amend the proposed rule to make all on-reservation acquisitions mandatory decisions. Retain discretion for off-reservation acquisitions but add cultural resources for the potential reasons that a tribe may acquire off-reservation lands within their aboriginal area.

68

LETTER SUBMITTED FOR THE RECORD BY WILLIAM IYALL, CHAIRMAN

COWLITZ INDIAN TRIBE,
LONGVIEW, WA 98632–8594,
OCTOBER 3, 2013.

Hon. DON YOUNG, *Chairman,*
House Subcommittee on Indian and Alaska Native Affairs,
1324 Longworth House Office Building,
Washington, DC 20515

Hon. COLLEEN HANABUSA, *Ranking Member,*
House Subcommittee on Indian and Alaska Native Affairs,
1324 Longworth House Office Building,
Washington, DC 20515

Re: Cowlitz Indian Tribe Comments for Subcommittee Oversight Hearing on Executive Branch Standards for Land-in-Trust Decisions for Gaming Purposes

DEAR CHAIRMAN YOUNG & RANKING MEMBER HANABUSA:

On behalf of the Cowlitz Indian Tribe ("Cowlitz Tribe" or "Tribe"), I submit these comments on your subcommittee's September 19, 2013 oversight hearing on off-reservation acquisitions of land into trust for gaming. The Cowlitz Tribe respectfully requests that these comments be included in the record of the hearing.

During the hearing, there was discussion regarding whether section 20 of the Indian Gaming Regulatory Act (IGRA), 25 U.S.C. § 2719, and implementing regulations in 25 CFR part 292 should be amended to curb what some characterized as the unchecked proliferation of off-reservation Indian casinos. The Cowlitz Tribe stands with the vast majority of Indian tribes in opposing any amendment to section 20 of IGRA, and agrees with the Obama administration that it is unnecessary to revisit the part 292 regulations promulgated in 2008. The reasons are simple: the unchecked proliferation of off-reservation Indian gaming is a myth, and the Obama administration, as well as the Bush administration that preceded it, already has made it exceedingly difficult for Indian tribes to acquire off-reservation land in trust for gaming through policy implementation and through the criteria laid out in the part 292 regulations.

The September 19 oversight hearing focused on a specific exception to the prohibition on gaming on lands acquired in trust after October 17, 1988: the so-called "two-part determination" exception contained in section 20(b)(1)(A) of IGRA, 25 U.S.C. § 2719(b)(1)(A). But we believe that any proposed legislation to amend section 20 of IGRA is unlikely to be limited only to that exception, and instead may seek to make unnecessary changes to some of the other section 20 exceptions, in particular the remedial exceptions for restored lands and initial reservation. As we explain below, there are important policy reasons underlying these remedial exceptions to the prohibition on gaming in section 20 of IGRA which counsel against their further restriction or amendment.

IGRA was enacted in 1988 "to provide a statutory basis for the operation of gaming by Indian tribes as a means of promoting tribal economic development, self-sufficiency, and strong tribal governments." The problem was that not all tribes held tribal lands in 1988 and, in fact, not all tribes even enjoyed Federal recognition in 1988. For that reason, Congress included the restored lands and initial reservation exceptions in section 20, to assist such disadvantaged tribes by providing that, when they finally obtained recognition and land, their land would be treated as if it effectively had been in trust since before October 17, 1988. In other words, Congress provided a mechanism by which newly recognized or restored tribes would be on a more level playing field with the tribes that were fortunate enough to have been recognized and have a land base on the date of IGRA's enactment. Congress knew that preventing newly recognized and restored tribes from accessing the economic development opportunities made available by IGRA would do an incredible injustice to those tribes. Similarly, IGRA allows a tribe which receives replacement lands as part of a land claim settlement to use the replacement lands for gaming in order to ensure that the settlement land has the same gaming eligibility status as the lost pre-1988 land it is replacing.

The purpose and intent of IGRA's restored lands and initial reservation provisions are informed by the opinions of the Federal courts that have considered these exceptions. In 2003, in a case involving a California tribe, the D.C. Circuit (in an opinion joined in by now Chief Justice Roberts) explained that the restored lands and initial reservation exceptions "serve purposes of their own, ensuring that tribes lacking reservations when IGRA was enacted are not disadvantaged relative to more established ones." *City of Roseville* v. *Norton,* 348 F.3d 1020, 1030 (D.C. Cir. 2003). In 2002, in an opinion involving a Michigan tribe that was later affirmed by the Sixth Circuit, the District Court said nearly the same thing, saying that the term "restoration may be read in numerous ways to place belatedly restored tribes in a comparable position to earlier recognized tribes while simultaneously limiting after-acquired property in some fashion." *Grand Traverse Band of Ottawa and Chippewa Indians* v. *U.S. Attorney for the Western District of Michigan,* 198 F. Supp. 2d, 920, 935 (W.D. Mich. 2002), *aff'd* 369 F.3d 960 (6th Cir. 2004) (referring to the factual circumstances, location, and temporal connection requirements that courts have imposed). The restored lands provision "compensates the Tribe not only for what it lost by the act of termination, but also for opportunities lost in the interim." *City of Roseville,* at 1029.

From a public policy standpoint, the need for special assistance for newly acknowledged and restored tribes is clear. Newly recognized and restored tribes have had to function without a land base and/or without formal Federal recognition for very long periods of time. Almost by definition, these tribes—tribes like the Cowlitz Tribe—have been more disadvantaged and have suffered greater hardships than those which have had trust lands and access to Federal assistance for many years. The remedial exceptions in IGRA section 20 address these disadvantages.

Nevertheless, the remedial exceptions have not been frequently used over the history of IGRA, and the Bush administration adopted implementing regulations in 2008 (25 CFR part 292) that impose even further restrictions on the application of these exceptions. For example, satisfying the regulatory requirements for the initial reservation exception in 25 CFR § 292.6 is a rigorous task that requires thousands of pages of documentation. To qualify for this exception, a tribe must meet the following criteria: (i) it must be federally recognized through the Bureau of Indian Affairs' (BIA) administrative acknowledgment process; (ii) it cannot have a gaming facility on newly acquired lands under the restored land exception in IGRA section 20; (iii) its land must be taken into trust and proclaimed a reservation and must be the first proclaimed reservation following acknowledgment; (iv) if the tribe does not already have a proclaimed reservation, the tribe must demonstrate the land is located within the State where the tribe is now located, as evidenced by the tribe's governmental presence and tribal population, and within an area where the tribe has significant historical connections and one or more of the following modern connections to the land: (1) the land is near where a significant number of tribal members reside; or (2) the land is within a 25-mile radius of the tribe's headquarters or other tribal governmental facilities that have existed at that location for at least 2 years at the time of the application to have the land taken into trust.

The Cowlitz Tribe is intimately familiar with these rigorous requirements. The Tribe was federally acknowledged on January 4, 2002 through the BIA administrative acknowledgment process. The Tribe emerged from the acknowledgment process with no reservation land base but the Tribe immediately submitted a fee-to-trust application for approximately 152 acres of land in Clark County, Washington. The Tribe has fought for the last 11 years to obtain these reservation lands and engage in economic development on them. In 2010 and again in 2013, the Department of the Interior determined that the land should be acquired in trust and that it satisfied the "initial reservation" exception found in section 20 of IGRA. 25 U.S.C. § 2719(b)(1)(B)(ii). Unfortunately, litigation to overturn the Department's decision has further postponed the Cowlitz Tribe's efforts to achieve tribal self-determination and economic development for its members. Given the Cowlitz Tribe's experience, the notion that there is unchecked proliferation of off-reservation Indian gaming, or that there is a need to make more stringent the criteria for newly recognized tribes to acquire land in trust for gaming, simply bears no relation to reality.

For the foregoing reasons, the Cowlitz Tribe urges the subcommittee to refrain from introducing legislation to amend section 20 of IGRA or to insist on even more onerous regulatory requirements for trust land acquisitions for gaming—these are likely to make it all but impossible for disadvantaged tribes to ever reach a level playing field with tribes lucky enough to have functional land bases when IGRA was enacted. On behalf of the Cowlitz Tribe, I thank you for the opportunity to share our views with the subcommittee on this important matter.

Sincerely,

WILLIAM IYALL, CHAIRMAN,
Cowlitz Indian Tribe.

PREPARED STATEMENT OF DRAGONSLAYER, INC. AND MICHELS DEVELOPMENT, LLC

Dragonslayer, Inc. and Michels Development, LLC (together, the Cardrooms) hereby submit this testimony for inclusion in the record of the September 19, 2013 House Committee on Natural Resources Hearing on "Executive Branch standards for land-in-trust decisions for gaming purposes."

The Cardrooms submit this testimony regarding concerns over the objectivity and sufficiency of compliance with the National Environmental Policy Act (NEPA) review conducted by the Bureau of Indian Affairs through its consultant, Analytical Environmental Services (AES). The Cardrooms have first-hand experience on this issue through the NEPA process for the Cowlitz Tribe's trust land acquisition for a casino and our review and understanding of NEPA documents for other tribal trust land acquisitions. This problem has been very evident in the effort of the Cowlitz Tribe to acquire land in trust and obtain an initial reservation for a 152-acre parcel adjacent to I–5 near La Center, Washington where we maintain our businesses. The proposed casino is opposed not only by us, but also by Clark County, Washington, the city of Vancouver, Washington, local citizen groups, landowners, and other tribes. The land at issue was owned at the time of the initial request in 2002 by a powerful tribal member who would benefit from the development of the site by his tribe. He is now in a business relationship with two other Indian tribes, one from Connecticut and one from California, to develop the casino once the land is placed in trust. The Cardrooms are currently in litigation against that development, along with the parties noted above. The litigation raises many issues that go to the heart of Federal Indian policy under the Indian Gaming Regulatory Act (IGRA), including the question about whether a post-1934 tribe like the Cowlitz qualifies for trust land under *Carcieri* Supreme Court decision, *Carcieri* v. *Salazar,* 555 U.S. 379 (2009).

One of the legal issues in our litigation concerns the objectivity and sufficiency of the environmental impact statement (EIS) prepared for the Bureau of Indian Affairs (BIA) by AES. After litigating BIA's failure to release documents held by AES in its role as the NEPA contractor for BIA, we obtained records via a Freedom of Information Act request that reveal that the Cowlitz Tribe exercised virtually day-to-day control over the EIS. BIA played virtually no role. We raised this concern in a letter to BIA on December 17, 2010, included as Exhibit 1 to this testimony. BIA looked the other way despite the problem of improper influence raised in our letter. This experience raises strong concerns over BIA's failure to oversee NEPA compliance and the ability of tribes to have a strong and improper role in deciding the contents of an EIS. This is very evident in the Cowlitz decision, where the EIS failed to consider alternative sites within the Tribe's historic land base north of the La Center, Washington site that is owned by the gaming financial backers.

We have identified another common problem with gaming EISs—in this case those prepared by AES for various tribes—of avoiding any true consideration of alternatives beyond the site preferred by the tribe. For example, in the Cowlitz FEIS, AES considered the Tribe's preferred site, one offsite alternative located near a school and hospital, and rejected 11 offsite alternatives, including those within the Tribe's own land base area as determined by the Indian Claims Commission where it maintains housing and government facilities.

Other EISs prepared by AES for BIA reveal the same pattern of constraining the decisionmaker by limiting alternatives. In fact, several recent EISs prepared by this consultant show the same pattern used for the Cowlitz proposal—the Tribe's preferred site and plan is used as the proposed action, with alternative scenarios for development of that site, no or only one "strawman" offsite alternative, which typically is undesirable for clear reasons, and other promising offsite alternatives "eliminated from further consideration" based on a cursory description. *See, e.g.,* Enterprise Rancheria FEIS (considers only the Tribe's preferred location, and one alternative that cannot be developed, three other reasonable sites rejected); Graton Rancheria FEIS February 2009 (Tribe's preferred site, one offsite alternative, 12 offsite alternatives eliminated); Ione Band FEIS February 2009 (Tribe's preferred site, no offsite alternatives, one offsite alternative eliminated), Spokane Tribe FEIS 2012 (only three alternatives considered for development at the preferred locations, five offsite alternatives all on land already owned by the Tribe rejected from further consideration). As these examples illustrate, NEPA review for Indian casinos, at least as prepared by AES, appear to follow a pattern of leaving BIA with no choice other than to select the Tribe's preferred location. Coupled with BIA's lack of supervision and the extensive and improper role granted to tribes to decide the content of EISs, BIA's trust land process for casinos is seriously flawed.

We believe that the solution to many disputes over IGRA casinos lies in selecting alternative sites that have consensus support. An EIS should facilitate the identification of such alternatives, not rule them out for the goal of supporting the tribes' or a casino backer's preferred result. BIA should ensure that its EIS documents meet this NEPA requirement, and not simply allow consultants paid by casino proponents to make such decisions after extensive communication by the very parties who benefit financially from selection of the proposed location. It is time for serious reform of NEPA compliance for gaming-related trust land requests.

We respectfully request that this committee investigate BIA's NEPA compliance for casino development projects. Thank you for considering our point-of-view.

———

LETTER SUBMITTED FOR THE RECORD BY GLENDA NELSON, TRIBAL CHAIR

ENTERPRISE RANCHERIA
ESTOM YUMEKA MAIDU TRIBE,
OROVILLE, CA 95966,
OCTOBER 2, 2013.

Subcommittee on Indian and Alaska Native Affairs

Re: Oversight Hearing on "Executive Branch standards for Land-in-Trust Decisions for Gaming Purposes" September 19, 2013 at 2:00 p.m.

DEAR CHAIRMAN YOUNG, RANKING MEMBER HANABUSA, AND MEMBERS OF THE SUBCOMMITTEE:

My name is Glenda Nelson, and I write on behalf of our 900 tribal citizens as Chairwoman of the Estom Yumeka Maidu Tribe of the Enterprise Rancheria ("Enterprise" or "Tribe"). In September 2011, Assistant Secretary-Indian Affairs Larry Echo Hawk issued a favorable two-part determination for 40 acres of land that we had requested to be taken in trust for gaming purposes in Yuba County, California. In August 2012, California Governor Brown concurred in the two-part determination. Shortly after the Department of the Interior ("DOI") issued its final decision to take the land in trust in November 2012, the Cachil Dehe Band of Wintun Indians of the Colusa Indian Community ("Colusa") challenged the Secretary's decision in Federal court. The Federal judge assigned to the case subsequently denied the request for a temporary restraining order, and the 40 acres were placed in trust for the Tribe in May 2013.

Colusa recently provided the subcommittee with oral and written testimony expressing its concerns with DOI's implementation of the Secretarial two-part determination process. We feel a response to the testimony is necessary to address several of the unsupported and false claims made by Colusa, to provide a better understanding of the unique circumstances that led to DOI's decision, and to explain why we believe the process is working as intended.

DOI's decision to take land in trust for our Tribe followed an exhaustive and comprehensive process that lasted over a decade. That process allowed project opponents—including Colusa and a few other tribes that object to our project for competitive reasons—multiple opportunities to weigh in and voice their concerns. Colusa, however, failed to take advantage of the opportunities to comment, did not respond to the BIA's request to submit comments, and remained largely silent throughout the DOI's administrative process that led to the decision which Colusa now so vehemently opposes. For instance, we cannot identify a single comment made by Colusa on the draft or final environmental impact statement ("EIS") even though Colusa now claims that the socio-economic analysis was deficient and that the widely respected environmental contractor used by the Bureau of Indian Affairs ("BIA") to assist in the EIS preparation, which Colusa and dozens of tribes have also relied upon for their expertise, was somehow biased. Obviously, DOI cannot be expected to address alleged deficiencies in the EIS analysis without comments, particularly given that Colusa controls the proprietary information required to determine whether the competitive impacts analysis in the EIS could have been improved.

Similarly, while Colusa's testimony suggests that it was excluded from the two-part consultation process by regulations that do not define a "nearby tribe" broadly enough, the facts show otherwise. Colusa never responded to the attached letter from the BIA in July 2009 providing Colusa information related to our trust application and two-part request and inviting Colusa to "submit comments and/or documents that establish that your governmental functions, infrastructure or services will be directly, immediately and significantly impacted by the proposed gaming establishment." Colusa never provided the DOI with the economic impacts analysis that Colusa cites in its testimony. That is not surprising: the analysis was prepared in 2013, well after DOI had made its two-part determination in September 2011. Nor is there any indication in Colusa's testimony that Colusa commented on the proposed 25-mile designation for "nearby tribes" during any of the extensive tribal consultations or comment periods offered over several years as part of the rule-making for the 25 CFR part 292 regulations issued in 2008 (even though our project was publicly announced in 2002). Instead, Colusa ignored the extensive consultation that occurred to develop the regulation and simply cites to the 50-mile radius set forth in the DOI's guidelines issued in 2000, without consultation, and then asks the subcommittee to compare that with the 25-mile radius established in rule-making by the Bush administration after multiple consultations with tribes. Regardless, the fact of the matter is that Colusa, despite any distance radius, was invited by the BIA to submit comments on our project and it declined to do so.

Colusa's testimony is replete with judgments about what Enterprise should or should not have done to engage in gaming. The testimony is particularly hurtful given that our Tribe reached out several times to Colusa very early on in this process to discuss these issues on a government-to-government basis, but Colusa declined to meet with our Tribal Council. Colusa's testimony is also disappointing because Enterprise has long enjoyed good relations with Colusa, is impressed by Colusa's efforts to use gaming as a means to first jumpstart and then diversify its tribal economy, and respects the sovereign rights of each and every tribe. We simply want the opportunity to exercise the same rights that Colusa has enjoyed for the past 30 years. We consider it our responsibility to promote self-sufficiency for the current and next generation of our tribal citizens by properly exercising our rights under Federal law.

Like other California tribes, Enterprise was rendered landless in the 1850s after the Senate failed to ratify the 1851 treaties and enacted legislation requiring the settlement of all land claims within 2 years. In an effort to remedy the circumstances of the surviving bands of homeless Indians, in 1915 and 1916 Federal agents purchased two 40-acre rancherias for our Tribe with funds appropriated by Congress. The rancherias were located near the town of Enterprise in the foothills above Oroville in Butte County, California. In 1964, Congress authorized the sale of one of the two rancherias to the State of California for construction of the Oroville Dam. That rancheria now lies under the waters of Lake Oroville. While the other 40-acre rancheria escaped a similar fate, it is simply too remote, steep, culturally sensitive, and difficult to access to serve as anything more than the site for a few residences. Representatives of DOI and the Governor's Office who visited the rancheria prior to their respective decisions have concluded as much.

Certainly if Enterprise had been blessed with a viable land base to establish even a modest gaming facility, we would not have spent the last decade seeking to acquire new trust land and qualifying it for gaming under section 20 of IGRA. Because my father refused the overtures by Federal agents to terminate our land and rights as Indians, our Tribe was never terminated. Consequently, Enterprise could not rely upon the more streamlined, less scrutinized restored lands exception that three neighboring tribes have used to qualify their new trust lands—located 11, 15, and 25 miles respectively from those tribes' former rancherias—for gaming. Instead, our only option was to acquire land and have it taken in trust and deemed eligible for gaming under the seldom-used and more stringent two-part process fraught with the practical and political uncertainties of a discretionary Secretarial determination, a lengthy environmental review, and a Governor's concurrence.

Fortunately, in 2002, we were able to identify an appropriate site for development of a gaming facility. Contrary to Colusa's claims, the 40-acre site is located within our historical area in the Feather River drainage basin, about 32-miles from our tribal offices, and about 5 miles from the Tribal health clinic that we operate-with two other Maidu tribes in Yuba City. As you know, Colusa testified and acknowledged that our project site, is not located in Colusa's ancestral lands. Further, the site is ideally suited for the development of a gaming facility in that it is located near an 18,000-seat amphitheater in an area zoned by Yuba County voters for sports and entertainment.

We were also fortunate to find a developer willing to risk his own capital to fund this 10 plus year effort. Although Colusa argues that the developer will be the primary beneficiary of our gaming facility, this is expressly prohibited under IGRA. We fully are aware that in the first few years of operation, the most tangible benefit for our tribal members will be the creation of jobs and training opportunities. Over time, however, we expect that the facility will generate sufficient revenues to allow us to greatly expand our tribal governmental programs and services. In addition, our gaming facility will provide significant benefits to one of the most economically disadvantaged regions in the Nation. In addition to providing jobs and economic activity, we have entered into various agreements to mitigate project impacts on the local community. Fortunately, our tribal-State compact commits a portion of our

73

gaming revenues for payment of those local agreements, with the remainder going for payments to non-gaming and limited-gaming tribes throughout California.

We are extremely proud of being only the third tribe in California and only the sixth or seventh in the Nation to have a project approved under the section 20 two-part process. While Colusa argues that our two-part determination will result in a flood of requests by other poorly situated tribes in California or by gaming tribes simply seeking a better location, the evidence strongly suggests otherwise. Most of the decisions made by DOI over the past few years have been made on requests submitted a decade ago when developers were willing to invest in tribal gaming projects, and DOI has denied as many projects as it has approved. Further, issuance of the section 20 regulations under 25 CFR part 292 and DOI policy guidance has resulted in not only more, but clearer and more stringent standards, particularly in respect to distance and historical ties. Few non-gaming tribes in California can identify an economically viable location and still satisfy these standards. For these and other reasons, no tribe in California has submitted a two-part request for a number of years. The process simply takes too long, is too expensive, and is too fraught with political uncertainty to attract the investment necessary to pursue the process. Thank you for your consideration.

Sincerely,

GLENDA NELSON,
Tribal Chair.

United States Department of the Interior

BUREAU OF INDIAN AFFAIRS
Pacific Regional Office
2800 Cottage Way
Sacramento, California 995825

WAYNE R. MITCHUM, SR., *Chairman,*
Colusa Indian Community Council,
Cachil Dehe Band of Wintu Indians,
3730 Highway 45,
Colusa, California 95932.

DEAR MR. MITCHUM:

We are in receipt of your letter dated June 23, 2009 regarding the Enterprise Rancheria's request to have 40.00 acres of real property in Yuba County accepted into trust.

In your letter, you stated your opposition to the Enterprise Rancheria gaming application in Yuba County and would like to be consulted with as a nearby tribe. You also requested a copy of the fee-to-trust application and the two-part determination application for the Enterprise Rancheria. Enclosed is a CD with the scanned copy of the fee-to-trust application, the two-part determination request and supplemental documents.

Although pursuant to 25 CFR part 292, you do not qualify as a nearby tribe for purposes of consultation under this part, you may submit comments and/or documents that establish that your governmental functions, infrastructure or services will be directly, immediately and significantly impacted by the proposed gaming establishment.

For further assistance on this project, please contact Arvada Wolfin.

Sincerely,

AMY L. DUTSCHKE
Acting Regional Director.

CITY OF KENOSHA,
KENOSHA, WI 53140,
OCTOBER 3, 2013.

Office of Congressman DON YOUNG,
2314 Rayburn House Office Building,
Washington, DC 20515

Re: Menominee Kenosha Project

DEAR MR. YOUNG:

Recently the Sub-Committee on Indian and Alaskan Affairs held a hearing to review the criteria used by the Bureau of Indian Affairs in its acquisition of trust lands for Indian Tribes. At the hearing there was discussion of the recent decision by the Assistant Secretary for Indian Affairs regarding the acquisition of trust lands for the Menominee Indian Tribe of Wisconsin.

As Mayor of the city of Kenosha where the lands to be acquired on behalf of the Menominee Indian Tribe are located, I can assure you of the overwhelming support of the local community for acquisition of these lands on behalf of Menominee. Both the City and County of Kenosha have passed resolutions in favor of the acquisition on behalf of Menominee. Both City and County citizens have approved of the acquisition on behalf of Menominee through referenda. The City and County have entered into a comprehensive Intergovernmental Agreement with the Menominee Indian Tribe regarding the acquisition.

I would note that the Federal process of approval of the Menominee acquisition has taken over 9 years and has been extremely thorough. After careful analysis of information provided by many sources, including those arguing against the acquisition, the Department arrived at a very well supported conclusion that the acquisition is in the best interest of the Menominee Tribe, and not detrimental to the local community. It is a decision in which I concur.

I appreciate the opportunity to provide my views on this issue and request that this letter be included as testimony for the September 19,2013 subcommittee hearing.

Sincerely,

KEITH BOSMAN,
Mayor.

PREPARED STATEMENT OF THE TOWNS OF LEDYARD, NORTH STONINGTON AND PRESTON, CONNECTICUT

The Towns of Ledyard, North Stonington, and Preston, Connecticut (Towns) hereby submit this testimony for inclusion in the record of the September 19, 2013 House Committee on Natural Resources Hearing on "Executive Branch standards for land-in-trust decisions for gaming purposes."

Our Towns are uniquely situated to provide testimony on the issues associated with Indian gaming, including trust land, off-reservation casinos and gaming-related facilities, taxation of non-tribal personal property on reservation lands, and tribal acknowledgment that is propelled primarily by the interest in casino development under the Indian Gaming Regulatory Act (IGRA). Our experience comes from decades of serving as the last community for the reservation and casino of the Mashantucket Pequot Tribe (MPT), from many years of participation as interested parties in the tribal acknowledgment procedures for the Eastern Pequot and Paucatuck Eastern Pequot petitioner groups, and from recent litigation with the MPT over its claim that non-tribal slot machine vendors who lease gaming equipment for use at the Foxwoods resort are exempt from slots and local personal property tax. *Mashantucket Pequot Tribe* v. *Town of Ledyard,* 722 F.3d 457 (2d Cir. 2013). In all of these matters, our Towns have successfully defended our local residents from the inappropriate application of Federal law. Our litigation against the Department of the Interior beginning in 1995 to challenge off-reservation trust land expansion resulted in the withdrawal of the MPT application in 2002 and the successful and cooperative use of that land under local land use laws. In 2005, the Department of the Interior properly denied the Eastern Pequot and Paucatuck Eastern petitions. And recently, the Second Circuit ruled 3–0 that non-Indian slot machine companies must pay personal property tax like any other business that maintains such property on reservation lands. *Id.* The MPT has sought rehearing on this decision. *Mashantucket Pequot Tribe* v. *Town of Ledyard,* No. 12–1727 (filed Aug. 21, 2013).

Based on this experience, we are deeply troubled by recent policy initiatives from the Department of the Interior. These actions appear to be poised to re-open long-settled matters, stir up new conflicts and controversies, and create new rules or policies that lack balance and objectivity.

One such action is the shortsighted proposal by BIA to rescind the 30-day wait period following any trust land decision. Land Acquisitions: Appeals of Land Acquisition Decisions, 78 Fed. Reg. 32,214 (May 29, 2013) (to be codified at 25 CFR part 151). BIA promulgated the rule for this wait period in 1996, in part in response to our MPT trust land litigation. It provides an important waiting period before the transfer of title that guarantees for local governments and other parties the fair opportunity to seek a consensus outcome with the tribes involved or, if necessary, to pursue its day in court.

At the same time BIA is pursuing their proposal, it announced an intention to withdraw the so-called self-stay policy, under which BIA has for nearly 20 years informally agreed to not transfer title to trust land that is subject to litigation. The policy has had a positive effect for all parties by avoiding the need for preliminary injunction litigation, encouraging negotiation, and reducing conflict. Our Towns have explained these issues in written comments, set forth in Attachment 1.

We also are concerned by actions by BIA intended to do an end-run around the U.S. Supreme Court decision in *Carcieri* v. *Salazar,* 555 U.S. 379 (2009). Again, this ruling had its origin in our 1995 MPT litigation, where the complaint raised the argument that post-1934 tribes are not eligible for trust land under section 5 of the Indian Reorganization Act (IRA). It is clear from actions by BIA in other contest that an effort is being made to devise legal arguments under section 5 that undermine the law of the land as set forth by the Supreme Court.

A third troubling procedure in law ruling the current administration is to approve off-reservation tribal land for gaming purposes. Such action used to be the exception to the rule and allowed only when local governments agreed with such actions and were covered by intergovernmental agreements. Now, it appears that virtually every off-reservation trust land agreement for gaming purposes is approved, regardless of the conflict or controversy.

Finally, in what may be the most egregious development yet, the Assistant Secretary for Indian Affairs, Kevin Washburn, has proposed sweeping changes to the tribal acknowledgment rules that would very significantly lower the test for petitioners to gain Federal tribal status and limit the rights of third parties to participate, as we did in the Eastern Pequot and Paucatuck Eastern Pequot petitions. This proposal is so extreme it would virtually automatically reverse the negative findings in those and other Connecticut petitions. The proposal calls into question the serious question of whether Congress has even conferred such power on the Secretary. Our comments on the acknowledgment proposal are set forth in Attachment 2.

Thank you for considering this testimony. We urge the committee to take such action as is necessary to restore balance and fairness to the administration of these laws and policies.

———

PREPARED STATEMENT OF THE CITY OF MEDFORD, OREGON

The city of Medford, Oregon appreciates the committee's effort to review the standards the executive branch is applying to gambling-related trust decisions. The acquisition of land in trust for casino development has tremendous impacts on the host community beyond the loss of taxing and regulatory authority. Casino development fundamentally alters communities, bringing traffic, noise, crime, and other adverse impacts, even with careful coordination and mitigation.

Given the significance of trust decisions, the Department of the Interior should strictly apply the regulatory standards that govern such decisions. There are heightened concerns when the trust application is combined with a gambling eligibility decision. Unfortunately, the Department appears inclined to approve any application it receives, without regard to regulations, the standards the Department has previously applied, or the impacts its approval will have on affected communities or the Indian tribes the Department purports to serve. Not only does the Department appear willing to approve applications without careful scrutiny, the Department is working at the same time to change its trust regulations to reduce notice and opportunities to participate and to loosen tribal acknowledgment criteria, which will further the proliferation of casinos.

Something must change with respect to how these proposals are evaluated. Applications by tribes that already have casinos, in particular, should be scrutinized much more carefully and the Department should put a far greater emphasis of the views of the surrounding community. Second, third and even fourth casinos should be permitted rarely, if at all, and only when there is unanimous support for the development.

The Oregon Situation

The City recognizes that each State must decide for itself how it will address the expansion of tribal casino gambling within its borders. In Oregon, the State long ago adopted a policy of "one casino per tribe." Oregon thus believes there must be clear limits on the Department's ability to expand casino gambling within Oregon's borders and has worked to ensure that casino gambling does not proliferate in the State.

This policy has worked for Oregon and Oregon tribes for two reasons. First, Governor Kitzhaber has supported each of the State's nine federally recognized tribes' pursuit of Class III casino gambling by giving the tribes wide latitude on the types of gambling permitted and the proposed size of the casinos. But recognizing that unfettered expansion of casino gambling would be harmful for the State and Oregon tribes, Governor Kitzhaber limited its expansion by negotiating compacts that are site-specific and circumscribing the circumstances under which a tribe may negotiate another Class III casino.

The second reason for the policy's success is because the Department—at least with respect to Oregon tribes-has largely complied with the Indian Gaming Regulatory Act's (IGRA) prohibition on gambling on newly acquired lands in section 20 of the act, 25 U.S.C. § 2719(a). In the past, the Department has permitted gambling under an exception to section 20's prohibition on gambling on newly acquired land only when the applicant tribe did not already have a casino and could show a strong historical and modern connection to the area. When a tribe could not meet these requirements, the tribe pursued a new casino pursuant to the two-part determination process in IGRA, 25 U.S.C. § 2719(b)(1)(A).

The Oregon tribes have adhered to that policy for years, which has resulted in a relatively stable gambling market and strong intergovernmental relationships that have developed in a climate of trust. In Oregon, tribal investments in gambling casinos are not routinely jeopardized by efforts made by other tribes to leap-frog over existing facilities to more favorable locations. In other words, Oregon tribes have not faced the type of undercutting that tribes in California, Oklahoma, Washington and Wisconsin apparently face, as was discussed during the September 19 Oversight Hearing.

The witnesses at the Oversight Hearing made clear how devastating some of the off-reservation proposals will be and the reasons that the Department should have denied the requests. In fact, much of the testimony focused on how the Department has been administering the two-part determination test and the apparently lack of standards for issuing a "no detriment" finding. Under the two-part determination, gambling is permissible on newly acquired land only if the Secretary determines that (I) gambling will be beneficial to the tribe and (2) not detrimental to the surrounding community *and* the Governor of the affected State concurs in that determination. The witnesses expressed concerns regarding how the Secretary was making the "no detriment" determination, because in many cases, it appears that the impacts on the surrounding community would be extraordinarily detrimental.

The Medford Application Exemplifies the Misuse of the Exceptions to Section 20

How the Department is making the "no detriment" determination is not the problem in Oregon (at this time). Rather, the issue Medford faces is getting the Department to apply the two-part determination test in the first place.

In passing IGRA, Congress attempted to balance the needs of tribes to engage in economic development with the concerns of State and local government regarding unregulated gambling expansion within their borders. The Department of the Interior and the Department of Justice were similarly concerned with the expansion of gambling off-reservation and how States and tribes would be affected.

To address those concerns, Congress created exceptions to put landless or newly-acknowledged tribes on "equal footing" with tribes that already had trust or reservation land when Congress passed IGRA. Under the "equal footing" exceptions, gambling is permissible if the land qualifies as land: (1) obtained as part of a land claim settlement; (2) designated an initial reservation of a tribe acknowledged by the government; or (3) as the "restored lands" of a restored tribe.

For cases when an exception did not apply, Congress included the two-part determination process as an alternative route. The two-part determination process is supposed to balance legitimate local concerns with the applicant tribe's goals of promoting tribal economic development and tribal self-sufficiency. Recognizing that in such situations the applicant tribe would be straying from its historic lands or adding to an existing land base, Congress gave States and local governments a more significant role than in "equal footing" cases. Thus, if a tribe wants to develop a casino off-reservation, it must work with the affected local governments, the community, neighboring tribes and the State to gain their support before an off-reservation casino can be approved.

There are certainly times where one of the three "equal footing" exceptions should apply. The Medford proposal, however, is not one of those cases. This past year, the Coquille Indian Tribe announced that it wants to turn a bowling alley in Medford into a Class II casino. The Coquille Tribe *already has* a Class III casino—the Mill Casino—which is located on Highway 101 in North Bend, overlooking Coos Bay. The Mill Casino offers over 700 slot machines and Vegas-style table games, including black jack, roulette and craps, and opened for business on May 15, 1995. The tribe expanded the casino just 5 years ago when it opened the Hotel Tower, which added 92 rooms including 6 suites, an executive suite, pool and hot tubs, a fitness center, 5 new meeting rooms and a full-service banquet kitchen. The tribe also has a 6,512-acre reservation located in southern Coos County, mostly in and to the southeast of the Coos Bay-North Bend urban area and manages approximately 5,400 acres of forest in Coos County, Oregon. The tribe maintains its governmental offices, its health clinic, its housing authority and its member services in North Bend.

The city was very surprised to hear that the Coquille Tribe had purchased land in Medford for another casino. Not only was its proposal against the State's "one casino per tribe" policy, the tribe has no historical connection to Medford. In fact, Medford is a 170 miles from North Bend—a 3 hour drive. Medford is actually the historic territory of the Rogue River Indians. The Coquille Tribe's historic territory is not even in adjacent territory. Land immediately to the northwest of Medford is the historic territory of the Umpqua (Cow Creek Band) and land to the west was Chasta, Sco-ton, and Grave Creek territory. The Medford site is far-flung land, does not qualify for an exception, and should be processed under the two-part determination process.

The Department has, for years, applied a test to impose limits on the application of the restored lands exception-one which would preclude the Coquille Tribe's request for a restored lands finding for Medford. That test looks at the factual circumstances of the acquisition, the location of the acquisition, and the temporal relationship of the acquisition to the tribal restoration. In practice, land will not qualify as restored lands unless the tribe has significant historical and modern connections to the site and the tribe has prioritized the acquisition of the land, as demonstrated by long-standing efforts to obtain the land beginning soon after restoration.

The Medford site does not meet this test. The tribe' presence in Medford is negligible, at best, and falls far short of the significant historic and modern connections the law requires. For more than 17 years, the tribe has operated a casino in North Bend and has thousands of acres of land located in the vicinity for its reservation. Its governmental services are all located near North Bend, as are its economic ventures. Medford is a 3-hour drive away from all of the tribe's existing development, activities and government. In fact, the North Bend site itself qualified as "restored lands" almost two decades ago. The tribe has shown no interest in Medford until this past year when it assessed Medford as a potentially lucrative site for a casino.

There is no basis for allowing the tribe to qualify for the "restored lands" exception twice, 170 miles from home, when it already has a casino. The Coquille Tribe's argument is based on a misreading of the regulations, which were never intended to apply in the fashion that the Coquille Tribe argues and which a judge for the Eighth Circuit has expressly rejected. The exceptions are not supposed to provide a loophole to enable a tribe to avoid the two-part determination process. The Coquille Tribe is seeking special advantage, not "equal footing," and the Department should not permit it.

The Application, If Approved, Will Have Enormous Impacts on Oregon and Nationally

This application has generated tremendous controversy and has impacted our relationship with the tribes that are part of our community. The tribes in whose historic lands this casino would be built are deeply distressed by the Coquille Tribe's proposal. The City has met with the Cow Creek Band of Umpqua Tribe of Indians, the Shasta Indians, descendants of the Rogue River Indians, and others to discuss the Coquille Tribe's application and proposed casino, and all believe that it is simply unacceptable to allow a tribe with no historic connection to Medford to have land acquired in trust in the city and declared eligible for gambling as "restored lands."

The Coquille Tribe knows that, given the Governor's "one casino per tribe" policy, the chances of obtaining a gubernatorial concurrence through the two-part determination process are very slim. Rather than abide by the State's policy, or attempt to work with the State to address concerns, the tribe has asked the Department to cut Medford and the State out of the process. The Coquille Tribe's attempted use of the "restored lands" exception would not only expand the application of that exception well beyond anything that Congress intended or that the Department have ever previously granted, it would also strip the State, the affected jurisdictional governments, and nearby tribes of critical procedural protections, including the gubernatorial concurrence requirement, that is required if the Department were to apply the legally required two-part determination process. Thus, the city is concerned not just that the Department is making "no detriment" determinations against the overwhelming opposition of the surrounding communities and affected tribes, but that it is helping tribes avoid the process altogether.

The question that remains is whether the Office of Indian Gaming will grant the tribe's request. The city has reached out to the Department to discuss its concerns, but the Department has not responded to the city's repeated requests for a meeting. Mr. Washburn testified before the committee that he has never refused a meeting request from a tribe, but he apparently will not even respond to such requests if made by a local government.

If the Office of Indian Gaming approves the tribe's request, the Department will create a loophole for other, similarly situated tribes and deprive Medford of the procedural protections Congress granted it. The effect of the Department allowing the Coquille Tribe to go forward under the exception should not be underestimated. While the Coquille Tribe has characterized its application as "only" for a Class II casino, the critical question is whether the land is eligible for gambling. And if it is eligible for gambling, the next step will be to negotiate with the State for a Class III casino, with the threat of suit if the State does not oblige.

Moreover, Oregon tribes are also likely to begin to seek additional land for at least Class II gambling, with an eye down the road to expand to Class III. In fact, Medford has already been informed that if the Coquille Tribe's application is approved, the Cow Creek Band will have to file its own request because a Medford casino will jeopardize the investment the Cow Creek Band has made in its reservation lands by undercutting its casino. The State will face more applications, in and around the metropolitan areas and along the I–5 corridor. What is now a relatively stable gambling environment will be irreparably altered by this single request of the Coquille Tribe to evade the two-part determination process, if the Department permits this abuse.

The city of Medford requests that the committee look closely at the Department's treatment of gambling-related requests. It should focus not only on how the Department is applying the two-part determination test, but also at how it evaluates the applicability of an "equal footing" exception. It will do little good to tighten the two-part process only to have the Department loosen the standards that apply to the exceptions, as the Coquille Tribe has requested. The Department should be prohibited from determining that land acquired in trust qualifies for gambling under one of the three exceptions if that tribe already has trust land and is operating a casino. To permit the exceptions to be used in the manner the Coquille Tribe advocates, or in any similar manner when a tribe already has land and casino development, is an impermissible expansion of the "equal footing" exceptions.

Moreover, the City believes that the Department should not be permitted to issue a "no detriment" finding and acquire land for gambling purposes over the opposition of the surrounding community. Gambling development has proven to be a boon for some tribes, but there comes a time when gambling expansion must be measured against the impacts on the communities and neighboring tribes, and those impacts must be realistically considered. Permitting tribes to build ever more casinos, without regard to the views of the host community and the neighboring tribes is a race to the bottom. The ultimate loser will be the tribes the Department is supposed to help.

The city thanks the committee for its work and hopes that its oversight of this issue will help protect States, communities like the city of Medford, and the tribes that have made investments with the expectation that Department of the Interior will apply gambling standards reasonably and fairly.

LETTER SUBMITTED FOR THE RECORD BY CRAIG CORN, TRIBAL CHAIRMAN

MENOMINEE INDIAN TRIBE OF WISCONSIN,
CHAIRMAN'S OFFICE,
KESHENA, WI 54135–0910
OCTOBER 3, 2013.

Office of Congressman DON YOUNG,
2314 Rayburn House Office Building,
Washington, DC 20515

Re: Menominee Indian Tribe of Wisconsin—written testimony, House Committee on Natural Resources: Subcommittee on Indian and Alaska Native Affairs, Oversight Hearing: Executive Branch Standards for Land-in-Trust Decisions for Gaming Purposes.

DEAR CHAIRMAN YOUNG:

As Chairman of the Menominee Tribe of Wisconsin, I am writing to correct some misunderstandings that were evident in statements made in the September 19, 2013 hearing conducted by the Subcommittee on Indian and Alaskan Native Affairs regarding the Department of the Interior's determination that acquiring land for the Menominee Indian Tribe in Kenosha, Wisconsin would be in the best interest of the tribe, and not detrimental to the local community. I would like to take this opportunity to provide some pertinent facts to the subcommittee so that these misunderstandings can be corrected.

1. The land to be acquired for the Menominee Indian Tribe in Kenosha, Wisconsin is not near any other Tribe's reservation. The closest trust lands to the site belong to the Forest County Potawatomi Community. Those trust lands, however, were acquired by the United States under the exact same provisions of law that apply to the Menominee acquisition. The Forest County Potawatomi Community's reservation is over 200 miles from the land to be acquired on behalf of the Menominee Indian Tribe.

2. The concerns and comments of both the Forest County Potawatomi and the city of Milwaukee were provided to the Bureau of Indian Affairs and taken into consideration by them in making their decision. This is not a situation where the Bureau of Indian Affairs ignored comments from those opposing the project. Rather, after taking those comments into consideration and carefully analyzing all the facts, it was determined that any impacts to the city of Milwaukee or the Forest County Potawatomi would be minor and short term.

3. The Forest County Potawatomi Community has approximately 1,400 members. Its off-reservation casino in Milwaukee, Wisconsin, according to press accounts, presently generates approximately $370 million in revenue annually. The largest negative impact to that revenue stream caused by the acquisition of trust lands for Menominee in Kenosha, Wisconsin projected by any credible study is 20 percent. Therefore, even under the worst case scenario, the Milwaukee casino would still generate approximately $300 million in revenue annually after the Kenosha casino began to operate. This equates to approximately $215,000.00 annually per Forest County Potawatomi Tribal member.

4. The Department of the Interior is not a rubber stamp for off-reservation acquisitions of land. The Menominee Indian Tribe can testify to this with great authority. The Tribe filed its application in 2004 and received approval in 2013. The hurdles tribes must overcome to obtain approval from the Department under the current regulations are extremely high. In 25 years since enactment of IGRA, only 8 tribes—including the Forest County Potawatomi Tribe—have been authorized to conduct off-reservation gaming under the 2-part determination procedure.

5. The acquisition on behalf of the Menominee Indian Tribe enjoys the overwhelming support of the local community as demonstrated by resolutions of support from the City and County where the lands are located, and favorable referenda by the citizens of the city and county where the lands are located. The project will create over 3,000 jobs and contribute significantly to the local economy. The tribe entered into an intergovernmental agreement with the city and county to mitigate any possible impacts and to provide for services to the planned facility.

6. The situation of the Menominee Tribe is truly unique. As discussed in detail in Interior's decision, the tribe has significant unmet needs due in large part to the lingering impacts of the tribe's termination in the 1950s. The gaming project will help the tribe meet those needs. Menominee County (which is coterminous with the reservation and 90 percent of its population are tribal members) is the poorest county in Wisconsin, with the highest unemployment and worst health indicator.

The Menominee Tribe would appreciate the subcommittee's consideration of these facts, and asks that this letter be entered into the record of the subcommittee's hearing of September 19, 2013.
Sincerely,

CRAIG CORN,
Tribal Chairman.

————

LETTER SUBMITTED FOR THE RECORD BY VINCENT DURO, VICE CHAIRMAN

SAN MANUEL BAND OF MISSION INDIANS,
HIGHLAND, CA 92346
SEPTEMBER 18, 2013.

The Honorable DON YOUNG,
Chairman,
House Indian and Alaska Native Affairs Subcommittee,
1324 Longworth House Office Building,
Washington, DC 20515

The Honorable COLLEEN HANABUSA,
Ranking Democrat,
House Indian and Alaska Native Affairs Subcommittee,
1324 Longworth House Office Building,
Washington, DC 20515

Re: Oversight Hearing: "Executive Branch Standards for Land-in-Trust Decisions for Gaming Purposes."

DEAR CHAIRMAN YOUNG AND RANKING MEMBER HANABUSA:

On behalf of the San Manuel Band of Mission Indians, a federally recognized Indian tribe based in southern California, I respectfully offer this testimony concerning the issue of off reservation land acquisitions for gaming.

For centuries, indigenous Serrano people occupied the San Bernardino and San Gabriel Mountains and their southern foothills, the Mojave Desert near Apple Valley to areas north of Barstow, and territories as far east as Twentynine Palms and Yucca Valley. The tribe, whose people are the Yuhaviatam, or "People of the Pines," is one of several clans of the greater Serrano Indian Nation. Today, the San Manuel Indian Reservation is located in a much smaller area along the steep foothills of the San Bernardino Mountains, consisting of approximately 950 acres over which the San Manuel tribal government exercises governmental jurisdiction.

In 1986, San Manuel first established gaming on our reservation as a tool for generating revenues for our tribe. Tribal government gaming has proven to be a useful tool for tribes to enhance our governance capabilities and become more self-sufficient with viable economic development efforts. Gaming has provided resources for tribes to more effectively protect their sovereign rights where they have come under increasing threat. It has provided tribes with the opportunity to focus on revitalizing tribal languages and cultures where poverty made survival the first obligation for many Indians. It has given tribes opportunities to reacquire lands that were sold or taken from them in more desperate days and make them a part of tribal territory once again.

Without a doubt, reacquiring aboriginal lands for many tribal communities is essential to efforts to rebuild themselves. There is much work to be done for most tribal communities to ensure that their homelands are protected and sustainable into the future. However, the efforts to acquire lands—especially those located far from existing reservations—bring added scrutiny to land acquisition and make such reacquisition efforts more difficult. Reacquiring land to build new schools, health centers or homes for tribal members today receives a higher level of suspicion largely because of fears that the land will be used for gaming projects.

Casino deal land acquisitions are not a new idea but one that has been refined, in a number of cases, by clever casino developers. The new pattern is non-Indian casino developers matching tribes with economically depressed, non-Indian communities in efforts to pull together a casino deal. Oftentimes, the tribe's existing reservation and the non-Indian community are miles and miles apart. With such deals, there can be hidden costs to non-Indian communities seeking short-term economic relief who are ill equipped to adequately assess the entities and individuals they are partnering with. This is a hard lesson learned by some Indian tribes.

There is now such a casino deal in the works within San Manuel's aboriginal territories in the California city of Barstow. The Barstow deal would allow the Los

Coyotes Band of Cahuilla and Cupeño Indians based in San Diego County to build a casino more than 160 road miles from its reservation, within Serrano historical territory. San Manuel has cultural resources in the Barstow area that we continue to monitor and take care of when necessary. These proposed casino deals and ones similar to them have the added effect of creating enormous tension between tribes who have claims to these lands as their aboriginal homelands as well.

Unlike some tribes, we believe that market protection is not a sound basis for Federal decisionmaking on land acquisition for gaming. Land is the anchor of our existence as sovereigns. Gaming is just one activity that stems from that sovereign existence.

We were pleased when the Department of the Interior acknowledged that tribes seeking land off reservation should have "significant historical ties" to the land for the Department to approve a proposed Secretarial, or two-part, determination. However, this policy position regarding connections to lands has changed from one administration to another, and has created great uncertainty particularly for the tribal nations.

President George W. Bush concluded that lands must be within a commutable distance from the existing reservation to the proposed site for the lands to be considered for a positive determination under the Two-Part exception. President Barack Obama has issued several positive determinations that have cited significant historical connection to the land as factors, but appears to have largely dismissed commutable distance as a point for consideration,

The San Manuel Band of Mission Indians has maintained that historical ties to the land under the Two-Part IGRA exception should be a requirement. This policy, if consistently applied, would establish a clear standard that demonstrates respect for traditional notions of tribal land areas. Any Departmental decisions, or decisions by the Congress to address this issue, should continue the sound policy of respecting aboriginal or historical ties to land,

We urge the subcommittee to support efforts of Indian tribes to protect their aboriginal lands from encroachment by tribes who cannot demonstrate significant historical connections to the lands being sought for gaming and other purposes,

Sincerely,

VINCENT DURO,
Vice Chairman.

PREPARED STATEMENT OF SPOKANE COUNTY, WASHINGTON

EXECUTIVE SUMMARY

Spokane County ("the County") strongly opposes concentrated development of any sort at the Airway Heights site, where the Spokane Tribe ("the Tribe") would like to develop an off-reservation casino-resort. The Tribe's 145-acre parcel is an exceptionally poor location to build an entertainment venue intended to attract thousands of visitors. Every hour, day and night, military aircraft fly less than 1,000 feet overhead the proposed casino-resort site as they approach the Fairchild Air Force Base's ("FAFB's") single runway, located 8/10 of a mile away. FAFB's military maneuvers and training operations, which include touch and go approaches, acrobatics, recovery operations, and other activities, are a critical component of our national security. FAFB is responsible for a variety of missions, the most prominent of which is its refueling mission, which relies on the massive KC135-Stratotankers. The wake turbulence produced by the KC135 is so disruptive that it can cause loss of aircraft control or catastrophic structural failure, so much so that small aircraft operating within 1,000 feet below are directed to stay at least 5 miles behind. Ex. 1 (FAFB Mid-Air Collision Avoidance Brochure). The site is not an appropriate place to build a casino, a hotel, a convention center, a mall, or any other type of development that brings large numbers of people potentially into harm's way and virtually ensures conflicts with FAFB's activities down the road.

The County has a number of obligations to its citizens. Those obligations include, first and foremost, protecting the public health and safety. Those obligations also include providing important public services, including transportation planning, road development, controlled urban growth, environmental preservation, considered economic development, recreational opportunities, and other services. The Tribe's proposed project will impair the County's ability to meet its obligations and will jeopardize the County's interests as a whole, detrimentally impacting the region.

It is the County's considered judgment that concentrated development located 0.8 miles from the FAFB's runway, immediately below the landing pattern, presents immediate health hazards and creates the potential for a catastrophic event that the

County is not equipped to handle. Without question, employees of the casino-resort, suppliers and visitors alike will experience repeated vibration, fumes, and noise disturbances. In addition, the FAFB's operations will be affected by the lighting a 24-hour casino-resort will require, undermining base operations and creating risks to pilots. While crashes are rare, they do occur and have occurred at FAFB. The risk of a catastrophic crash at the casino-resort development is far greater at its current location than in locations not immediately within FAFB's landing pattern. The risk of a disaster alone is great enough to warrant denial of the proposed location. The County would never permit such concentrated development at the proposed location, by any applicant.

A critical priority for the County is to protect the continued viability of FAFB itself. In fact, the State requires the County to do so. Ex. 2 (citing RCW 37.70.547 of Washington's Growth Management Act, which requires towns, cities, and counties to discourage development of incompatible land uses adjacent to public use airports through adoption of comprehensive plan policies and development regulations). The County sought to have FAFB located in the region, and business leaders contributed land for the purpose of winning the Base for Spokane. FAFB has been a strong and valued member of the community, one that the region invited and needs to protect. The economic benefits of FAFB cannot be overstated. Closure of FAFB would cause up to 12,085 job losses, a decline in population of 27,244, and an estimated loss of over $1.29 billion in total economic output to the County. The area tribes would be affected too, with anticipated combined losses to the tribal casinos estimated at $10,850,000. Because of its importance and pursuant to State law, the County has sought to prevent any activities that would encroach on the FAFB's operations, which include "any human activities or decisions that impair or may potentially impair the current or future operational capability of an installation complex or may have an adverse effect on nearby communities." Developing a high-density casino-resort, including a 145-foot tower, 0.51 miles from FAFB, constitutes encroachment. Tens of thousands of people would congregate at the casino resort. The facility would generate significant lighting and traffic impacts that interfere with FAFB's operations. These impacts have not been mitigated. For example, even with proposed mitigation such as downward cast lighting, glare impacts will be significant due to reflection, particularly during periods of snow cover. The County will take whatever steps necessary to protect the FAFB's current and future operational capability.

The Tribe has not contacted the County in its official capacity to discuss the possibility of an agreement or methods to mitigate the impact of its proposed casino-resort. The Bureau of Indian Affairs ("BIA") predicated the 2003 acquisition of the site in trust for the Tribe—over the objections of the County—on the commitment of the Tribe to work with the County to address jurisdictional conflicts and other concerns. The BIA stated its expectation that the Tribe would work with the County going forward and that concerns would be adequately addressed. The Tribe has not lived up to that expectation, and the Secretary should not excuse it from doing so. None of the impacts on the County-which stands to see its costs increased by several million dollars a year to maintain its current level of services to the community (assuming no impacts to FAFB)—have been mitigated. Thus, the County and the community it represents will be negatively impacted by development of the proposed casino.

The overwhelming opposition to the proposed project from almost every local government, State representative, community leader, and tribe in the region are further evidence of the detrimental impacts that this project will have on the community. Only two entities support the project: the Tribe itself and Airway Heights, whose approximately 6,138 residents (which includes a 2,500-strong prison population) expect to receive a minimum payment of $600,000 per year. The remaining 475,600 area residents are opposed, as demonstrated by the opposition by their representative leaders, and would receive no mitigation at all.

In light of thus reasoned opposition, the Tribe's request should be immediately denied. Respectfully, the Secretary has no basis for overriding the nearly unanimous views of the surrounding community regarding the detrimental impacts the casino-resort would have on the surrounding community. On issues of local land use and development, the local governments clearly know best what projects will detrimentally impact their communities. The Secretary does not have six decades of experience working with FAFB, does not know more than local leaders about the Spokane economy, and does not have sufficient experience with County operations to dismiss County objections. If the Secretary does overrule the community's views and approve the casino-resort, that action would be arbitrary and capricious. Further, if the Secretary is contemplating another outcome, the current environmental impact statement ("EIS") is an insufficient basis for decisionmaking. The purpose and need statement is impermissibly narrow, and, as a consequence, the "heart" of the document—the NEPA alternatives analysis—inadequate. Nor does the EIS properly evaluate the impacts the proposed project would have on the County, FAPB, or public health and safety. Moreover, since the EIS was completed, circumstances have changed. For example, the County rescinded the only agreement that provided any mitigation in order to free itself from a neutrality provision that prevented the County from expressing its views on the proposed casino resort, and because the mitigation proved to be inadequate once details of the proposal became clear. Additionally, after completion of Department of Defense-funded land use studies, local land-use regulations applicable to the casino-resort site have changed. This and other new information must be addressed in a supplemental EIS.

Additional review will only further underscore the detrimental effects the Tribe's proposal would have on the community. As set forth in the County's comments, there is no basis for allowing gaming on the Airway Heights site. The proposed project is fundamentally inconsistent with the training activities that take place directly overhead and near the proposed site and will have impacts that have not been mitigated. Although the County supports the Tribe's efforts to promote its self-governance capability, the Tribe's current proposal jeopardizes the economic' strength and stability of the very community on which the success of its proposal depends. A casino-resort at the Airway Heights site is not good for the County, FAPB, or the area tribes. The Tribe's request must be denied.

———

LETTER SUBMITTED FOR THE RECORD BY RUDY J. PEONE, CHAIRMAN

SPOKANE TRIBE OF INDIANS,
SPOKANE TRIBAL BUSINESS COUNCIL,
WELLPINIT, WA 99040
SEPTEMBER 18, 2013.

The Honorable DON YOUNG, *Chairman*,
Subcommittee on Indian and Alaska Native Affairs,
1324 Longworth House Office Building,
Washington, DC 20515

The Honorable COLLEEN HANABUSA, *Ranking Democrat*,
Subcommittee on Indian and Alaska Native Affairs,
1324 Longworth House Office Building,
Washington, DC 20515

Re: Spokane Tribe's Comments on Executive Branch Standards for Land-in-Trust Decisions for Gaming Purposes

DEAR CHAIRMAN YOUNG AND RANKING MEMBER HANABUSA:

I write to provide the Spokane Tribe of Indians' views on the issue of off reservation acquisitions of land into trust for gaming.

The Spokane people have inhabited northeastern Washington State since time immemorial. Our territory consisted of over 3 million acres of land that we protected and governed. Within this territory, we lived along the Spokane River in three bands known as the Upper, Middle, and Lower Spokane Indians. We fished the Spokane and Columbia Rivers and used the grand Spokane Falls as the principal permanent village of the Lower Spokane. In January of 1881, President Rutherford B. Hayes by Executive order established the Spokane Indian Reservation as the smaller home of the Spokane Indians. Today, the Spokane Tribe continues to govern its 157,000 acre Spokane Reservation that is based in Wellpinit, Washington, and is located about 50 miles from the city of Spokane that bears our name.

By the mid 1990s, the Spokane Tribe maintained two gaming operations on our reservation. Within a few short years, we were realizing the goal of tribal government gaming: that we would live with greater self-sufficiency. We were employing and educating our people, and we were able to provide better health care, education, and housing opportunities.

In 1999, the Department of the Interior issued a decision that devastated the Spokane Tribe's on-reservation economy. The Kalispel Tribe of Indians applied to have lands taken into trust and have those lands deemed eligible for gaming under the Indian Gaming Regulatory Act's Secretarial, or Two-Part, Determination, **in the heart of our tribe's ancestral territory and between the Spokane Reservation and the city of Spokane, far removed from Kalispel's ancestral lands.** In 1996, we informed Department of the Interior officials that Kalispel gaming in Airway Heights would devastate Spokane's distant, on-reservation gaming facilities.

To our dismay, the Department did not heed our concerns and our worst fears have come true.

Since the Kalispel Tribe opened its Northern Quest Casino in 2000, Spokane Tribe gaming revenue plummeted to a low of less than $20,000 in 2009. In 2009, employment on the Spokane Reservation declined by 13.6 percent raising the unemployment rate on the Reservation to 47 percent, up from 34 percent in 2008. In addition, 45.3 percent of those who are employed have such low earnings that they fall beneath the Federal poverty level. According to the 2000 Census, nearly one-quarter of families residing on the Reservation were living in poverty, compared with 11.7 percent in Stevens County and 7.6 percent in the State of Washington.

In direct response to the devastating impact of the Department's decision, in 2006 the Spokane Tribe submitted its application to have land already held in trust for the tribe deemed eligible for gaming under the Two-Part Determination. This land, located in the city of Airway Heights, between the Spokane Reservation and the city of Spokane, would bring economic relief to the Spokane Tribe and competitive parity with the Kalispel Tribe. Gaming revenues will enable the Spokane Tribe to provide basic governmental services that today eludes a membership suffering from dismal unemployment and high poverty rates. Beyond essential services such as health care, gaming revenues will enable the tribe to fund cultural preservation and language programs while addressing critical, on-Reservation natural resource issues. The project will create substantial employment opportunities for tribal members. The increase in tribal governmental capacity will create additional professional tribal governmental job opportunities for the membership. The project will also benefit the surrounding community, including the creation of nearly 5,000 jobs in a community marred by double-digit unemployment rates.

Sadly, Kalispel actively opposes the Spokane Tribe achieving this determination from the Department of the Interior. Kalispel leaders continue to argue that the Department of the Interior should protect the Kalispel Tribe's gaming market from competition from the Spokane Tribe. The Spokane Tribe's observations of the executive branch's consideration of fee to trust gaming applications are informed by the tribe's experiences with the devastating effects of reservation shopping and as a tribe with a gaming application currently under Department review.

THE 2008 REGULATIONS PROVIDE CLARITY, TRANSPARENCY AND STAKEHOLDER INPUT IN DEPARTMENTAL REVIEW OF TRIBAL GAMING APPLICATIONS.

The tribe stands with the vast majority of Indian country in supporting the Department's implementation of regulations governing determinations on gaming related fee to trust applications, which the Department promulgated in 2008 after formal agency rulemaking ("2008 Regulations"). The 2008 Regulations recognize important limitations on approval of tribal gaming applications and require transparent decisionmaking upon consideration of public comments, including NEPA compliance and a separate consultation process for State and local governments. To its credit, this administration has responded to Indian country's request to address a backlog of tribal gaming applications through careful application of the 2008 Regulations.

In March 2006, the Department initiated formal rulemaking for regulations to govern land into trust gaming decisions. As a general matter, IGRA prohibits gaming activities conducted on Indian lands that are taken into trust after the date of IGRA's passage (October 17, 1988). 25 U.S.C. § 2719. The limited exceptions to this prohibition are listed in 25 U.S.C. § 2719 and include the "contiguous lands" exception, the "restored lands" exception, the "settlement of a land claim" exception, the "initial reservation" exception, and the "two part determination' exception. The Secretary provided a draft of the proposed regulations to all federally recognized tribes and sought comment both by letter and at four public hearings across the country. The Department received 74 letters, presentations, and policy papers providing extensive tribal comments on these draft regulations even before they were published for public comment several months later.

Interior began the formal notice and comment period on the new "part 292" regulations on October 5, 2006. The tribal comments reveal overwhelming opposition to any tribe attempting to game within the exclusive ancestral lands of another tribe. *See, e.g. Comments to 25 CFR part 292 Draft Regulations,* 73 Fed. Reg. 98, 29354 (May 20, 2008), *passim.* After all, any tribe concerned about devastating impacts to its on-reservation gaming operations from such approvals need only look to Spokane's circumstances. A year and a half later, Interior promulgated its Final Rule, codifying its interpretation of 25 U.S.C. § 2719. The regulations implement this section of the Indian Gaming Regulatory Act ("IGRA") by articulating the standards that Interior will follow in interpreting the various exceptions to IGRA's general prohibition on gaming on lands acquired after October 17, 1988.

On July 18, 2010, then Interior Secretary Salazar issued a directive recommending a thorough review of the 2008 Regulations, including yet another round of consultations. During this second round of consultation, tribes overwhelmingly expressed support for the regulations and strongly encouraged the administration to go about the difficult business of rendering decisions on pending tribal gaming applications, many of which had been under review for several years. To its credit, this administration has not shirked from applying the 2008 Regulations to make decisions on several tribal gaming applications. Some applications have been approved while others have been denied. Some await gubernatorial concurrence—the ultimate check on Secretarial two-part determinations. In each case, the Department issued lengthy decisions pursuant to clearly articulated requirements and upon consideration of voluminous records including comments from the public, local units of government, State and Federal agencies and Indian tribes.

The 2008 Regulations are noteworthy both substantively and procedurally. Substantively, and consistent with the overwhelming number of tribal comments, the 2008 Regulations require an applicant tribe to demonstrate a "significant historical connection" to the proposed gaming site. The 2008 Regulations define the term "significant historical connection" as one in which "the land is located within the boundaries of the tribe's last reservation under a ratified or unratified treaty, or a tribe can demonstrate by historical documentation the existence of the tribe's villages, burial grounds, occupancy or subsistence use in the vicinity of the land. 25 CFR § 292.2. The 2008 Regulations require an applicant tribe to demonstrate a significant historical connection to qualify for the restored lands exception, the initial reservation exception. While IGRA does not require an applicant tribe to demonstrate a significant historical connection to the land to receive a positive two-part determination, the 2008 Regulations nevertheless require the Secretary to weigh the existence of a historical connection between an applicant tribe and its proposed gaming site as a significant factor in determining whether gaming on the proposed site would be in the best interest of the tribe and its citizens. *See,* Northfork ILD, p. 11. Significantly, since 2008, the Department has denied at least two applications because the applicant tribe has failed to demonstrate a significant historical connection requirement to the proposed gaming site. *See, e.g.* Guidiville ILD, Sept. 11, 2011 ; Scott's Valley ILD, May 25, 2012.

Demonstration of a significant historical connection profoundly affects the application process. For instance, in support of its current two-part application, the Spokane Tribe demonstrated that the project site lies at the heart of Spokane's federally adjudicated exclusive territory, only a few miles from principal permanent villages and key fishing sites. The tribe demonstrated that the project site lies squarely within an important dry land camas harvest area, in close proximity to permanent villages and thus a logical starting point for the critical springtime harvest. The Spokane documented its engagement with the U.S. Army in September 1858 at the Battle of Four Lakes, within a few miles of the project site. The Spokane documented that the subsequent Battle of Spokane Plains raged *across* the project site. The tribe was able to point to a wealth of archaeology that documents the presence of nearby permanent villages, burial sites and fishing stations. In sum, the significant historical connections requirement set forth in the 2008 regulations provides a much-needed geographic anchor to tribal gaming applications and enjoys strong support in Indian country.

The 2008 Regulations also impose significant procedural requirements on Departmental review of tribal gaming applications. Tribal gaming applications are now subject to a full-blown Environmental Impact Statement under the National Environmental Policy Act. Preparation of an Environmental Impact Statement ensures transparency in the decisionmaking process and provides significant opportunity for public, agency and local governmental comment on anticipated impacts and required mitigation. For instance, public input on the Environmental Impact Statement prepared for Spokane's Application spanned from August 27, 2009 through May 1, 2013. Seven cooperating agencies including Spokane County, the city of Airway Heights and the U.S. Air Force provided comments on the project. In all, the BIA considered and responded to over 300 comment letters.

In addition to the NEPA process, the 2008 Regulations require the BIA to notify all local units of government within a 25-mile radius of a project site to request comments on the following areas:

1. Information regarding environmental impacts on the surrounding community and plans for mitigating adverse impacts;
2. Anticipated impacts on the social structure, infrastructure, services, housing, community character, and land use patterns of the surrounding community;

3. Anticipated impact on the economic development, income, and employment of the surrounding community;
4. Anticipated costs of impacts to the surrounding community and identification of sources of revenue to mitigate them;
5. Anticipated costs, if any, to the surrounding community of treatment programs for compulsive gambling attributable to the proposed gaming establishment; and
6. Any other information that may assist the Secretary in determining whether the proposed gaming establishment would or would not be detrimental to the surrounding community.

The Spokane Tribe has worked diligently with the local governments in the area, and we have reached inter-governmental agreements with all of them. Beginning in 2007, the Spokane Tribe reached out to the city of Airway Heights and Spokane County to discuss mitigation of impacts associated with our project. Discussions over the years produced a tri-lateral, Intergovernmental Agreement in 2010 between the tribe, the city and the county regarding development on the proposed site. That agreement remains in effect today. However, after initially committing to remain neutral on the project, the composition of the County Board of Commissioners changed, and the currently comprised Board now opposes our project. The current Board recently chose to back out of an agreement with the city of Airway Heights that would have provided additional compensation to the county once gaming occurs on the site. Notably, the city remains contractually bound to the tribe to allocate a portion of the tribe's annual mitigation payment to the county. The tribe is confused by the county's recent arguments concerning lost tax revenues, since the county lost its taxing authority over the site when it was placed into Federal trust in 2001. At full build out, however, the project will generate millions in indirect local, county and State tax revenues as employees and vendors recycle gaming dollars through the local economy.

The County has provided input at every step of the tribe's project and in fact chose to participate as a Cooperating Agency in the NEPA process. Contrary to Commissioner Mielke's testimony, the administrative record documents the BIA's careful consideration of the County's comments and reflects changes to the project made in response to some, but not all, of the county's comments. Furthermore, Commissioner Mielke is wrong to suggest that the tribe promised it would not game on the site when it was taken into trust in 2001. Instead, the administrative record in support of the tribe's initial fee to trust determination demonstrates that the tribe expressly sought the property for economic development and would not rule out the possibility of gaming.

The tribe takes exception to Commissioner Mielke's portrayal of our project as a potential encroachment on Fairchild Air Force Base ("FAFB"). As a Cooperating Agency, the Air Force has been closely involved in the development of mitigation measures for the project. The law presumes that cooperating agencies can speak for themselves concerning impacts upon their jurisdictions and necessary mitigation measures. With valuable input from the FAA, FAFB and the Air Force, numerous mitigation measures have been incorporated into the project, including building height restrictions, prevention of hazardous wildlife attractants, building material requirements for noise attenuation, lighting mitigation such as glare reduction, and commitments from the tribe's government to acknowledge and to not complain of impacts arising from existing or future FAFB flight operations. Notably, throughout the extensive NEPA and separate consultation process, neither the Air Force nor FAFB have identified the project as an "encroachment" on base operations.

Finally, the extensive administrative record belies Commissioner Mielke 's suggestion that only 1 percent of the region's population supports the tribe's project. Instead, the project enjoys broad support from local elected officials, labor leaders and local governments, including the city of Airway Heights, which is the local jurisdiction that will be most impacted by our project.

We respectfully submit that the committee should beware of certain local governments who seek an effective veto over tribal gaming applications by requiring the Department to uncritically defer to their claims of detrimental impacts. IGRA does not provide local governments with such a veto.[1]

Instead, IGRA requires the Department to balance state and tribal interests in tribal gaming activities. With respect to tribal interests, Congress expressly prohib-

---

[1] The Secretarial Determination is unique among the exceptions in that the governor of the State in which the proposed gaming site is located has an effective veto over final approval. 25 U.S.C. §2719(b)(I)(A); 25 CFR 292.22, 292.23. Thus, a favorable Secretarial determination, while critical, is not the final step in the approval process: the governor of the State in which the gaming is to occur must also concur in the Secretary's Determination.

ited gaming on lands acquired in trust after October 18, 1988. Pursuant to IGRA and the 2008 Regulations, the Department applies heavy scrutiny to all tribal applications for off-reservation gaming on lands acquired after October 18, 1988 to ensure that they do not result in a detrimental impact to communities surrounding the proposed gaming site. In so doing, the Department seeks to avoid upsetting the intent of Congress in enacting IGRA, which balances the economic development interest of Indian tribes with the interests of States in protecting local communities from detrimental impacts. *Enterprise ILD*, p. 28–29; *North Fork ILD*, p. 46–47.

Ironically, tribes that received off reservation gaming approvals in the early days of IGRA (approvals that would not have survived the added scrutiny of the 2008 Regulations) are among the strongest opponents of certain pending tribal gaming applications. These tribes are afforded a full opportunity to express their opposition. For instance, Kalispel has committed tremendous economic, political and legal resources to oppose Spokane's application at every opportunity. The crux of Kalispel's opposition to the Spokane's application is simple—after a 14 year gaming monopoly in Spokane's territory, they do not wish to compete with the resident tribe. The inequities inherent in Kalispel's request to maintain its gaming monopoly manifest in the level of "hardship" Kalispel would suffer if Spokane were allowed to open. Even if Kalispel's worst case scenario regarding projected reduction in profits is correct, the Kalispel Tribe would still have 14 times more revenue available per tribal member for the provision of tribal government services and programs than are currently available to the Spokane Tribe.

Despite Kalispel's considerable opposition, the Spokane Tribe is confident that the Department will not act as a guarantor of Kalispel's gaming monopoly. In interpreting the 2008 Regulations, the Department has determined that "IGRA does not guarantee that tribes operating existing facilities will continue to conduct gaming free from both tribal and non-tribal competition." *Enterprise ILD, p. 32, citing Sokaogon Chippewa Community* v. *Babbit,* 214 F.3d 941 (7th Cir. 2000). That sound policy resonates in Spokane's case, in which a foreign tribe with no historic ties to the area seeks to preclude the resident tribe from fairly competing in a gaming market capable of sustaining both tribes. In any event, the 2008 Regulations have provided Kalispel ample opportunity to load the record with comments backed by studies from various consultants. Regardless of the merits of the decision on Spokane's application, Kalispel cannot fairly complain that it was denied the opportunity to have its comments considered by the Department.

The 2008 Regulations mark a sea change in Departmental review of off reservation gaming applications. Each post-2008 determination reflects the Department's careful review of all substantive comments submitted by the public, local governments, and State and Federal agencies. Each post-2008 Determination is the product of a transparent decisionmaking process that includes the benefit of an exhaustive NEPA analysis and consultation with local units of government. The current leadership within the Department is continuing this administration's commitment to process a backlog of difficult and nearly always controversial tribal gaming applications.

　　Respectfully,

RUDY J. PEONE
Chairman, Spokane Tribal Council.

––––––

PREPARED STATEMENT OF THE TOHONO O'ODHAM NATION, OFFICE OF THE CHAIRMAN AND VICE CHAIRMAN

Following is the written testimony of the Tohono O'odham Nation ("Nation") relating to the subcommittee's recent hearing titled "Executive Branch standards for land-in-trust decisions for gaming purposes." The Nation respectfully requests that this testimony be included in the record of the hearing.

On September 17, 2 days before the hearing, the House passed H.R. 1410. Entitled "The Keep the Promise Act of 2013", H.R. 1410 in fact reneges on the promises the United States made to the Nation in the Gila Bend Indian Reservation Lands Replacement Act (Pub. L. 99–503), Federal legislation which settled the Nation's land and water claims against the United States in 1986. Despite the fact that H.R. 1410 already had been voted on by the full House, both Chairman Young and Ranking Member Hanabusa took the opportunity once again to malign the Nation and its efforts to implement the settlement benefits that the United States promised to the Nation in the 1986 Federal settlement statute. Chairman Young remarked that: "[t]he passage of a House bill this week to block an off-reservation casino in Phoenix is a sign of popular support for taking the off-reservation gaming rubber stamp away from the administration, and letting Congress make decisions regarding gaming." Yet the Federal courts repeatedly have ruled that the Nation's effort to acquire certain land in trust and use it for gaming-related economic development is entirely consistent with Congress' existing direction in both the Nation's settlement statute and IGRA. Unfortunately, Ranking Member Hanabusa also ignored the Federal court decisions specific to the Nation's efforts, stating that: "[i]f enacted into law, H.R. 1410 would prevent any Arizona tribe from circumventing existing Federal authorities to conduct gaming off-reservations. I view that legislation an example of the safety valve Congress can provide when tribes seeks to engage in so-called reservation shopping ." It is deeply distressing that our Federal trustee continues to ignore the plain language of existing Federal law and the clear rulings of the Federal courts. The position taken by the committee on H.R. 1410 is in fact a total abdication of the United States' obligations to the Nation under its 1986 settlement act, and is reminiscent of the 1950s Termination Era.

This year marks the 25th anniversary of IGRA. In July, the National Indian Gaming Commission reported that in 2012 Indian gaming generated $27.9 billion. This economic development has been instrumental in affording tribes the opportunity to fund tribal government services, including healthcare, law enforcement, education, and cultural activities; it also has had a profound positive impact on surrounding communities, creating thousands of jobs for non-Indians. This economic development engine—which is not dependent on federally appropriated dollars—is particularly crucial during these difficult economic times. Accordingly, during a 2011 hearing before the Senate Committee on Indian Affairs, Chairman Stevens of the National Indian Gaming Association cautioned against amendments to IGRA: "[f]or hundreds of tribal governments there is simply too much at stake to open the Indian Gaming Regulatory Act up to amendments on the floor of either the House or Senate. Tribes have consistently opposed subjecting IGRA to amendments for the past 23 years."[1]

The September 19th oversight hearing focused on the so-called "two-part determination" exception contained in section 20(b)(1)(A) of IGRA, 25 U.S.C. § 2719(b)(1)(A). The Nation is concerned, however, that any proposed amendments to IGRA would extend to some of the other exceptions; in particular, IGRA's remedial exceptions in section 20(b)(1)(B). These include the settlement of a land claim exception (under which the Nation seeks to game and which H.R. 1410 would frustrate), the initial reservation exception, and the restored lands exception. 25 U.S.C. § 2719(b)(1)(B)(i)–(iii). Congress provided these limited remedial exceptions in IGRA in recognition of the historical wrongs experienced by those tribes that qualify for the exceptions, so that these disadvantaged tribes also could access the benefits of Indian gaming. The Department of the Interior has hardly implemented these statutory exceptions with a "rubber stamp"—the exceptions have been utilized only a very few times since IGRA's enactment, and currently they are rigorously applied according to Departmental regulations adopted by the Bush administration that further limit their application and scope. There is no question but that amendments to these exceptions in IGRA would disproportionately impact the most vulnerable tribal nations with the least resources, and would be contrary to the United States' trust responsibility to those tribes.

For these reasons, the Tohono O'odham Nation stands together with the administration, the National Indian Gaming Association, and many other tribal governments in opposing amendments to the Indian Gaming Regulatory Act. Any such effort would be ill-advised and detrimental to the economic well-being of tribal nations, States, and the surrounding communities who benefit from Indian gaming under its current legal and regulatory structure. The Nation urges the committee to be true to the original intent of the remedial exceptions, to recognize the historical injustices that the exceptions are intended to address, and refrain from imposing even more draconian limitations than already were put into place by the previous administration. Otherwise, the adverse effects of the committee's actions will disproportionally impact the most disadvantaged and vulnerable tribal nations.

The Tohono O'odham Nation thanks the subcommittee for this opportunity to share its views on this very important matter.

---

[1] U.S. Senate, Committee on Indian Affairs, The Future of Internet Gaming: What's at Stake for Tribes? 112th Cong., 1st Sess. S. Hrg. 112–490 (Nov. 17, 2011).

89

LIST OF DOCUMENTS SUBMITTED FOR THE RECORD RETAINED IN THE COMMITTEE'S OFFICIAL FILES

Cow Creek Band of Umpqua Tribe's Exhibit Book re Opposition to Coquille Indian Tribe's Proposed Medford Casino (within that book are the following submissions):

- Opposition letter from Oregon House of Representatives
- Opposition letter from Oregon Governor
- Opposition letter from Oregon General Counsel
- Opposition letter from Jackson County, Oregon
- Resolution and Opposition letter from City of Medford
- Report from EcoNorthwest re Application of Lottery Impact Methodology on the Case of a Casino in Medford
- Southwest Oregon Tribal Political Areas
- Historical Background: Report of Stephen Dow Beckham

○

www.ingramcontent.com/pod-product-compliance
Lightning Source LLC
Chambersburg PA
CBHW080317290526

45790CB00005B/2083

* 9 7 8 1 5 0 8 5 5 6 3 0 5 *